Distant Freedom

# Distant Freedom

## Essay on Chekhov

Jacques Rancière

Translated by Steven Corcoran

polity

Originally published in French as *Au loin la liberté* © La fabrique éditions, 2024



Polity Press
65 Bridge Street
Cambridge CB2 1UR, UK

Polity Press
111 River Street
Hoboken, NJ 07030, USA



ISBN-13: 978-1-5095-6734-8 – hardback
ISBN-13: 978-1-5095-6735-5 – paperback

A catalogue record for this book is available from the British Library.

Library of Congress Control Number: 2025946208

Typeset in 12.5 on 15pt Adobe Garamond
by Cheshire Typesetting Ltd, Cuddington, Cheshire
Printed and bound in Great Britain by Ashford Colour Ltd



For further information on Polity, visit our website:
politybooks.com

# Contents

## The Tramp's Dream

It is a story from 1886 titled *Dreams*, one among others that year, that made the young Anton Chekhov realize, with the help of a few privileged readers, that he was not just a satirical chronicler for small popular magazines but a real writer.

Yet it is, at first glance, the simplest kind of story imaginable: three men are walking along a road. We don't know where they set out from. And the story will end without them having reached their destination. The only factual event will have been a break. Their walk itself seems to refute any change of place. The muddy road their feet sink into is exactly the same ahead of them as it is behind them. And all around them a whitish fog forms a wall that closes off all perspective and accentuates the feeling of motionless tramping in a space indefinitely similar to itself.

Of course, there is a reason for their walking, and it is given to us in the first sentence, which, at first glance, sums up the whole story. A simple routine of country life: two constables are leading a tramp to town. The two constables are quickly characterized in the manner of a humorous storyteller: one is stocky and short-legged, the other long and straight as a stick. But here the trouble creeps in, and the smooth surface of this insignificant story is hollowed out by the character of the third man: this tramp who no longer remembers his name and looks like anything but a tramp.

Solving this twofold enigma, finding out why he cannot remember his name and why he bears so little resemblance to his character, thus provides the material for a new narrative that hollows out the uniformity of this walk on the spot: an investigation led by the short-legged man who answers to the name of Ptakha. Slowly and dreamily, as if he were talking to himself, the nameless tramp responds and provides the key to the double enigma: firstly, that of his appearance. He may have been born a peasant, the son of a serf, but his mother was a servant in a seignorial home and brought him up with a love of religion, of good manners and of refined language. And if he does not look like a peasant, it is because his father was probably a lord, the advances of whom his pious mother had been unable to repel. Things went badly wrong when the lord in question chose a new companion, which perhaps explains the pious mother's mistake of inadvertently pouring arsenic into the glass of medicine that the son took to the master every evening. This 'mistake' resulted in both mother and son being sent to a penal colony, from which the son escaped. That is why he had 'forgotten' his name. Knowing his name would condemn him to return to the penal colony to be among uncouth people, something unbearable for his delicate sensitivity, whereas, as a tramp, he would simply be deported to Siberia.

Over the course of the conversation, the nameless tramp turns out to be a character typical of modern fiction: an illegitimate child, part nobleman, part villein – but also an abridged account of the history of his country, the 'unwashed' land of slaves and lords stigmatized in a famous poem by Lermontov;[1] a land of vast social distances and illusory intercourses whose sovereign had,

[1] Прощай, немытая Россия,
Страна рабов, страна господ,
Farewell, unwashed Russia,
Land of slaves, land of lords.

twenty years earlier, abolished serfdom, yet without making freedom a reality.

Giving body to this freedom is the task the story will devote itself to by introducing a new fiction within the fiction. This fiction is the work of the tramp and consists in transforming the place of his destination. In his lyrical words, the Siberia of deportees becomes the land of freedom. The land there, he says, is vast and each person can have as much of it as they would like to sow, work and build on; the rivers there are broad and rapid, protected by steep banks and ancient fir trees, and countless fish swim there to the delight of fishermen who use lines and hooks, set creels or cast nets.

With this evocation of virgin lands of freedom, the simple story of the journey to the district capital is interrupted and the division of roles between the constables and the tramp is abolished. This is because the dream is also a reality – the agreement between a situation, the performance of a body and the landscape of thought that it gives rise to in people's minds. So long as the tramp speaks, his free country exists. The constables themselves, those men whose job it is to obey orders and lock people up, now share his dream; they paint themselves pictures of a life they have never known, but whose image has perhaps been passed on to them by distant ancestors or through time-honoured stories: that of the free man moving about unhindered in a free land of boundless steppes, wide rivers and tall fir trees.

At this point, where the fiction about the tramp gets lost in a dream about the free country, the very meaning of the journey and the distribution of roles are erased. The reality of his dream competes with the reality that the constables serve. One of them must thus make him fall silent and close the fictional parenthesis by re-establishing the simple story of the journey that takes a delinquent to the place of his sentencing. This is the natural role of the tall lean one. In a few words, he brings the dreamer of freedom back to the reality of the journey they have to complete, and to the reality of his own condition: he is a sick man, whom this short journey has already knocked the breath out of and who will drop dead of exhaustion long before he reaches the Siberia of his dream. With this simple call to order, images of the free country vanish from each of their three heads. But not its idea. And while the distinct images of the judicial process settle in the mind of the tramp, the constables' thoughts continue to wander: 'The constables are straining their imaginations to encompass what probably God alone can apprehend, namely the terrible expanse that separates them from the free country.'[2]

Let's not give God any more importance than he has in the prose of the unbelieving Chekhov. 'God alone can imagine', 'God only knows', 'God knows who': these expressions are often used by Chekhov, not to invoke the privilege

[2] Anton Chekhov, *Dreams*. Translator's note: In retrieving the Chekhov quotes for this book, I have consulted a good many of the various English translations of his work, notably those by Richard Pevear and Larissa Volokhonsky, Ronald Wilks and Constance Garnett. I have sought to render the English translations of these quotes to match the French ones given in this work as closely as possible, sometimes by mixing and matching the English translations, sometimes also by modifying them in accordance with the French rendering in this work, much of which is Rancière's own. There exists no standard or complete works of Chekhov's oeuvre in English, except in a unpaginated digital version. For this reason, I have generally not provided page references to the stories Chekhov quoted herein, with the exception of one of the plays, translated by Ronald Hingley, and Chekhov's letters, translated by Michael Henry Heim. The reader will find all the passages easily by searching in the freely available online version of the translation by Constance Garnett.

of divine omniscience, but to mark the limits of what the characters in the story are capable of identifying and understanding. The tramp's speech has broken with the straight path that, between two walls of fog, led straight to a place of confinement. It has split the space and time of the journey, placing at its fabulous origin and dreamt-of destination a point of reference that belongs to another order of magnitude: freedom. Freedom is situated at a distance that cannot be measured, but neither can one not seek to measure it. Even if the tramp has been stripped of the images of his dream, this dream now haunts the very order that condemns him. 'Right, time to go', says the constable. 'We've had our break.'[3] But the break is not over. It will remain inscribed in the uniform time of the journey as an irreparable breach.

Perhaps that is why the story, which seemed to take the characters on their way, now leaves them in the middle of the road. The story has an end because it stops. And it does not, because the characters have not reached the end of their route and we do not know what will happen to

[3] Ibid.

the tramp. This is, as we shall see, a constant feature of Chekhov's stories. Here it marks the short journey that goes from an arrest to a place of detention. But it will also mark the story of a love affair in *Ariadne* or *The Lady with the Little Dog*, and that of an entire life in *My Life* or *Three Years*. The advantage of the short story of *Dreams* is to allow us to perceive the discreet force that animates this way of telling: the feeling of an undecided opening up of time. The era of slaves and lords has been declared formally closed, and with it the uniformity of the repetitive time of servitude. Freedom has not yet arrived, but the new time is under the sign of its idea, and this idea can no longer be forgotten. This writer's task is to place us within its horizon, without lying about the distance that separates us from it or giving up on the demands it makes of us. It is to inscribe the rupture of distant freedom in the time of servitude.

**The Whirring of Servitude**

To do this, you first have to take the full measure of servitude. This writer's morality can be summed up in two simple, not to say simplistic, principles: the first is not to fear freedom. The second is not to lie. The truth is that freedom is frightening. If it is far away, it is because servitude is still very much with us, and firstly in our heads. It is indeed too simple to depict it simply in terms of the violence of the powerful and their police. It is firstly in the air we breathe and the effects it has on our minds: those of the constables and that of the tramp. In Lermontov's poem, unwashed Russia was the land of blue uniforms, of prying eyes and inquiring ears to which the people submitted with cowardice. But no reader of *Dreams* imagines that the constables really have prying ears that are likely to pass on the tramp's confidences to the judge. They do not threaten him or use violence. They simply order him to move on instead of dreaming. But they do not do so without experiencing the distance that separates them from the freedom whose dream they are taking away from him. Chekhov's Russia is not the empire of sadistic, knout-wielding officers that the Comtesse de Ségur née Rostopchine depicted for the young readers of *General Durakin*. It is the land of minds shaped by the memory of blows, given or received. In it, order reigns first through numbness. This is the lesson of the short story titled *In the Court*. A peasant accused of murdering his wife is astonished to find that the judges, jurors and courtroom audience exhibit neither 'threatening faces, nor indignant looks nor loud phrases about retribution'.[4] What can be seen on every face and in every attitude is simply the boredom of having to keep the judicial machine running, and the torpor caused by the tireless whirring of the fan that accompanies the clerk's dull voice and monotone recitation. Everything in the courtroom exudes peace. But the very peace that reassures the peasant is none other than the indifference of the administrative machine that condemns as a routine matter without having to be encumbered by any feelings of justice or hatred. Significantly, the story ends without letting us know the verdict. It closes with the normal course of the hearing resuming after the dodging of a revealing incident that could have called the whole prosecution into question. It matters little whether the accused is innocent or guilty. The important thing is that everything continues as if nothing had happened, as if nothing ever happened apart from the whirring of the ventilator and the administrative machine. This

[4] Chekhov, *In the Court.*

is servitude: not the submission of the common people to the representatives of order, but their common submission to the repetition of the same; not the obligation to obey, but the impossibility of imagining that things could be other than they are.

This impossibility or fear of imagining the slightest deviation from the order of things is embodied by one of Chekhov's most famous characters, the *Man in a Case*, Byelikov, anxious about what might happen every time his colleagues do something that no official circular forbids but none expressly authorizes. More than the ridiculousness of the character, we must pay attention to the cruel moral of the story. After the death of the schoolteacher, now locked in a case where nothing any longer risks happening to him, his colleagues feel for a moment like children on the loose. But before a week had passed, ordinary life resumes its course, a life just 'as gloomy, oppressive and senseless' as before – 'a life not forbidden by any government circular, but not fully permitted, either'.[5] Those who mock Byelikov forget that he is only the condensed image of the

[5] Chekhov, *Man in a Case.*

life they themselves lead, a life whose possibilities they do not believe they are allowed to explore.

This is the first legacy of serfdom: the fear of freedom, in other words, the impossibility of thinking that time can give rise to anything other than the identical repetition of the order of things. This is illustrated by a long novella with a singular title: *Three Years*, a title that announces no other content for the fiction than its own duration. A duration that is itself indifferent. These three years, which could be four or five without changing a single element of the story, are the condensed version of an existence destined to be forever similar to itself, an existence marked by the legacy of serfdom. Chekhov deliberately lent his hero, Alexis Laptev, a few characteristics from his own biographical history. Like him, he made him the grandson of a serf and the son of a merchant; like him, he was a child marked by the habit of paternal correction and the suffocating weight of religious rituals. No doubt the Laptev family's business was far more prosperous than Chekhov's father's own business and disburdened its heir of the obligation to work that weighed on the writer. But the dark building with its damp walls and narrow barred windows, where the father's bass voice droned on and on like the courtroom fan and where fifty employees shuffled about among boxes and crates, has all the appearance of a prison. And servitude is stamped on bodies and souls: on those of the employees, who are forced to live on the premises and be home by nine o'clock every evening; but also on those of the house's heirs, born to a mother terrorized by her husband, and marked by their father's daily inflicting of blows on them, similar to the inflicting of blows that their father had received from his own father, doubtless in memory of those the latter had received from his masters. This education in servitude made of Laptev a small, skinny individual, with a keen sense of physical insignificance. It also made of him a weak-willed person, fearful of anyone with the slightest authority: concierges and Swiss guards as well as police officers and gendarmes. Above all, it made him incapable of conceiving the possibility of happiness and of what for him is its concrete reality: shared love. That is why his story appears over before it even begins. When his beloved curtly rejects his declaration of love, he feels relieved that he no longer has to wait and hope, and can look forward to the quiet life of those who have only to follow the gentle descent of passing years: 'he needed to abandon all hopes of personal happiness, live without desires, without hopes, not dream, not expect . . . and then old age would approach unnoticed; life would come to an end – and nothing more was needed'.[6]

The story could end there, in the second chapter. If it has fifteen more chapters, it is because Laptev's renunciation is met with another one: that of the young girl, Yulia, who quickly feels the fragility of the apparently sufficient reason for her refusal. She does not love him. But, on second thoughts, the feeling of love appears so fleeting, and is perhaps important only in novels. In reality, there is marriage and family. And condition of this for a young girl is a reasoned choice between the possible parties. A quick scan of the available males in her provincial town, however, leads the sensible Yulia to conclude that the insignificant Laptev at least has the advantage of living in Moscow, of having studied and of knowing how to speak French. A marriage will therefore take place between this woman who has given up on love and this man who has given up on

[6] Chekhov, *Three Years.*

being loved. It will take place in the socially well-defined mode involving a commercial transaction between an ugly rich man and pretty poor girl.

In novels this kind of marriage leads to predictable misfortune: adultery and eventually suicide. But both Chekhov and his heroine have dispensed with the torments of the novel. Yulia, similar to Irina in *The Three Sisters* or the hero's wife in *The Fear*, enters into a simple contract with her husband: I do not love you, but I will be a faithful wife. Which also means: I will be a faithful wife if you do not make me love you. This contract of shared servitude excludes the great dramas of love and death for which the writer Chekhov himself has no appetence. These stories, he thinks, are the privilege of writers, sons of lords. The sons of shopkeepers, as far as they are concerned, do not build grand dramatic architectures; they just make nesting boxes for birds.[7] Everything will transpire, then, in the confines of a birdhouse. Laptev's only misfortune will be to live with a woman who does not love him and who relegates

[7] Ivan Bunin, *About Chekhov: The Unfinished Symphony*, edited and translated by Thomas Gaiton Marullo (Evanston, Ill: Northwestern University Press, 2007), p. 12.

him to the reality of his being a merchant and the grandson of a serf. Yulia will not cheat on her husband with any of his friends, the scientist Yartsev, the lawyer Kochevoi or the eternal student Kish. She would only form with them a small circle of shared discussions and amusements from which she would exclude him.

The story could end there. But the end is crueller in its very appearance of reconciliation. At the end of the famous three years, when his father's blindness and his elder brother's insanity have forced Laptev to take the reins of the family business, his young wife did not confine herself to simply assisting him. She would assure him of a love that, she says, his very absences have enabled her to feel. But rather than this declaration, which he was no longer expecting and to which his sensibility has long been dulled, Laptev thinks of the meal that awaits him. And, in fact, the love that his wife declares to him seems to be the upshot of the same mealtime-governing habit. So accustomed has she become to his presence that she suffers when he is away. The love she offers him is, at best, similar to the love that overcomes the hero of another short story, *The Teacher of Literature*, in which a respected teacher and young married man with a loving wife suddenly realizes the only possible way out of his 'happiness': 'I must escape from here, I must escape today, or I shall go out of my mind!'[8]

This temptation – Laptev had felt briefly, too. The previous evening, seated in the factory courtyard, having been informed of the thriving company accounts and realizing his inexorable future as the head of a great firm enslaved by his fortune, he overheard the passionate declarations and kissing of two unseen young people in the neighbouring garden. In a flash, he conceived the possibility of chucking in the business and its millions and leaving this oppressive place he had always hated: 'He went out into the middle of the yard, and, unbuttoning his shirt at his chest, gazed at the moon, and it seemed to him that he would order the gate to be unlocked, and would go out and never come back again. His heart ached sweetly with the foretaste of freedom; he laughed joyously, and pictured how exquisite, poetical, and even holy, life might be.'[9] There was only one gate to be opened. But Laptev did not

[8] *The Teacher of Literature.*
[9] *Three Years.*

pass through it. He remained standing there, in the yard, sensing what was preventing him from escaping: the habit of servitude – the servitude of habit – which paralyses the movements of his body just as it anaesthetizes the desires of his mind.

*The Teacher of Literature* ends without telling us whether its hero has taken the train to Moscow. It is clear, nevertheless, that Laptev will not be taking the main road. He will not even allow himself the day of freedom enjoyed by the student in *Bad Characters*, who sets off penniless in his hole-filled boots from his miserly father's house, and dreams at the same time of starving to death in the snow to shame his parents and of being welcomed into a house where his complaints will be listened to and where the young girl of the house will fall in love with him, before wisely returning home as some evening drizzle begins to fall. Before Laptev's eyes and in his head, there seems to be no other feeling than that of time passing. He observes its effects on his wife, who has blossomed, and his nieces, who have grown up over the last three years. And it is to her again that he turns when he thinks of the thirteen or thirty years he still has to live, before concluding with words of consent indifferent to the course of days and seasons: 'Let us live, and we shall see.'

### The Song of the Telegraph

The reluctant trader lets time take its course. But does time do anything? Does it go anywhere? The writer is not like his character. He cannot simply let time go by; he has to stand in places where time can be seen and shown to be at a standstill. Such is the embankment on which an anonymous narrator in *Lights* stands by chance one August evening: a character who has no more substance of his own than he has a reason to be there. We know two things only about him. The first, mentioned in passing, is that he is a doctor. The second is that he got lost on his way home from the fair. We will never know what he was doing there. But we do know that the fair is a favourite setting for the colourful tales of the great writer of the steppe, Nikolai Gogol. The lost doctor is, in a way, the writer who has deserted the universe of the colourful, gripping stories of his elder. For the latter, the short story was the time of unfolding of an entire world of sensations, but for this writer it is more like a random stop in a place where a singular case is encountered, a particular occurrence where the definite present of a life is measured against the indifference of time.

Thus, the lost traveller, who was looking for just one thing, a bed to sleep in, found himself welcomed by an insomniac engineer on a railway construction site. From the top of the embankment, amidst the chaos of mounds of earth and gravel, barracks, pits and wheelbarrows, dominated by the monotonous song of the telegraph wire, a privileged sight caught his eye: the long row of frozen and self-same lights that stretch along the track, eventually disappearing into the distant night. 'There seemed to be something in common between these lights, the stillness of the night and the disconsolate song of the telegraph wire. It seemed as though some weighty secret were buried under the embankment, and only the lights, the night and the wires knew of it.'[10]

This secret, buried beneath the embankment and known to distant lights, is the very secret of time. For the engineer Ananyev, this secret is an open book; it is the visible evidence of the fruits

[10] *Lights.*

of labour and of progress, which appears as a well-regulated forward march. A year ago, only bare steppe was there. Now there is life and civilization, represented by this railway line under construction. And, in a century or two, there will be what naturally follows the railways: the great trinity of buildings of enlightened, industrious and healthy modernity: schools, factories and hospitals.

Progress is there, visible in the long row of lights that pierce the night and audible in the engineer's enthusiastic words about this future borne of the very chaos of the present. The time limit for completion will undoubtedly be a long time in coming, but it is already anticipated by the body of the speaker, who appears to concentrate and to reduce its stages: 'His sunburnt, thick-nosed face and muscular neck seemed to say: "I am well fed, healthy and satisfied with myself, and the time will come when you young people too will be well fed, healthy and satisfied with yourselves".'[11]

This is the writer's privilege: to show this abstract future already visible on the body of the person who professes it, to show ideas insofar

[11] Ibid.

as they animate and sculpt bodies; but also, conversely, to shift the gaze towards the indecipherable chaos that undoes the evidence of these ideas and belies any presence of this future. On the embankment, which above all presents visitors with the image of an inextricable jumble, the writer has installed a third spectator who refutes the engineer's progressive vision. This is his assistant, the student Von Schtenberg. The first thing Von Schtenberg sees is the night into which the long row of lights disappears. And for him, this construction site of the workers of the future takes on the exact opposite appearance: it looks like a world long dead, a camp of those enemies of Israel (Philistines or Amalekites) whose very race has disappeared and whose fate presages that of the engineers of progress. 'So it will be with us. Now we are making a railway, are standing here philosophizing, but two thousand years will pass – and of this embankment and of all these men, asleep after their hard work, not one grain of dust will remain.'[12]

Another image of time, which is also the vision of a man from another generation. Ananyev's

[12] Ibid.

vision is faithful to the cult of science and progress shared by 1840s liberals and 1860s nihilists. The 1880s man, the student Von Schtenberg, came to embody a different kind of nihilism: no longer scientistic and revolutionary, but metaphysical and pessimistic. For the latter, history promises no liberating end. It is directed towards no end other than death. It brings peoples and civilizations into the light of day only to annihilate them and erase even their trace. It is like life, a blind force devoid of sense – meaning and direction. The student-engineer's argument thus radicalizes the disillusioned wisdom of the trader Laptev. The *qui vivra verra* reveals its nihilistic essence: *qui vivra mourra* – he who lives will die; from which point it matters little what he lives through or what he sees.

The engineer Ananyev thinks it does matter. So does the writer. But, of course, they do not grasp it in the same way. Ananyev is not Chekhov's spokesman. Chekhov will have none. He never says which of his characters he approves of. That is why his politicized colleagues readily accused him of what they deemed a sin against the spirit: indifferentism. In truth, he was by no means indifferent. He did not maintain an equal balance between antagonistic ideas. Quite simply, he did not weigh up ideas against one another. What he did was to give them another weight altogether by incorporating them into the movements of a body, the tone of a voice, the colour of a show or the tenor of a moment.

For the time being, he has the engineer Ananyev refute the young nihilist. Ananyev does it in the manner of mature men who use their experience to correct the abstract ideas of young people. He used to share these ideas, he says, but he saw to where they led. Thus, he recounts an episode from his life that has all the hallmarks of a novel, with its plot and its *dénouement*. Some time ago, he had been passing through his home town, meditating by the sea on the inanity of existence and the imbecilic force of life, when he thought it would be a good idea to find himself a woman, preferably a married one, for a fling to occupy the two or three days he had to spend there. At that very moment, chance found him the woman who was his high-school sweetheart, the young Kisochka, now suffering from an unhappy marriage. The plot was thus set in motion and, after a few incidents, Kisochka finds herself in Ananyev's hotel room that very evening. The only problem was that, for her, this move meant a definitive break with her husband and her past life, and the beginning of a new life of love. This misunderstanding forced the seducer, caught in his own trap, to leave clandestinely. The shame of this flight is to have taught the young Ananyev the damage caused by these great abstract ideas about the ultimate nothingness of things, which serve the most immediate and prosaic appetites.

The student remains unconvinced by the story. And the reader suspects that the narrator is similarly unconvinced. He himself finds it hard to understand how this fairly banal story of a cynical idler exploiting the credulity of a naive young woman can prove anything against Schopenhauer's philosophy. There is, in fact, an imbalance between this little personal adventure and the great thesis it claims to illustrate. By renouncing his nihilist ideas, Ananyev has proved nothing about the future of progress promised by hospitals, factories and schools. And, on this ground, the writer would have to give him slightly more formidable opponents than the student Von Schtenberg. We might think of the enthusiastic Likharev (*On the Road*), who was as passionate about science as he was about the workers, nihilism, the division of land, the Russian people, popular art and non-resistance to evil as truths to be propagated and to which he gave his life against all practical utility. But we might also think of his antithesis, the very rational Dr Ragin, who is the anti-hero hero of *Ward No. 6*. Ragin does not scorn science a priori. In the peace and quiet of his flat, he can be enthusiastic about the discoveries of Pasteur or Koch and the progress made in antisepsis. But science is also far away, as is freedom. How could the wonders of new scientific discoveries reach the hospital of a filthy little town, two hundred versts from the nearest railway? For science to restore the sick to health, there would have to be more medical equipment in it than two scalpels and a thermometer; the baths would have to be used for bathing the sick, not for storing sacks of potatoes; the superintendent, the housekeeper and the medical assistant would have to stop stealing from the sick; the municipal and regional authorities would have to give the hospital the means to provide real care; and the population itself would have to stop thinking that the wretched people confined in it are anyway better off there than at home. In short, if medical science is to help change the way people live and think, those ways of living and thinking must themselves have changed. Without this, the hospital, supposedly an instrument of progress, can be nothing other than a reflection of the stagnation and servitude that surround it. So, it is not his reading of Schopenhauer but his own experience that leads Ragin into the spiral of impotence and nihilistic resignation that will see him end up as a patient in the hospital where he was the doctor. What's the point in pretending to treat when you do not have the means to do so? And ultimately what is the point of treating people who are doomed to die anyway? For it to be worth helping them to live, life itself would have to be worth living.

Doctor Ragin's experience contradicts that of the engineer Ananyev far more radically than the borrowed philosophy of the student Von Schtenberg. But Chekhov carefully refrains from letting them meet. What is more, he provided the nihilist Ragin with a fiercer opponent than the enthusiastic Ananyev. This opponent is one of the patients under his care, a lunatic from *Ward No. 6*. This madman, it is true, is a formidable reasoner, and suffers from that madness of reasoning known as paranoia. But his paranoia has not simply fallen from the sky. It invaded the mind of this insignificant court usher called Gromov the day he came across two prisoners in irons in the street, escorted by four gendarmes. 'It suddenly seemed to him for some reason that he, too, might be put into fetters and led through the mud to prison like that.'[13] The law-abiding Gromov had doubtless never robbed or killed anyone. But how can we guarantee that he will not be guilty of such a crime one day, even if only inadvertently? How can we guarantee that he will not be slandered? That he will not be summarily tried by one of those courts knowing full well that everything that happens in them happens mechanically? That he will be able to make the voice of scorned innocence heard in this dump, located two hundred versts from the railway? From that day on, Gromov lived with the idea that his every word and gesture could land him in prison, and as a result he developed a series of aberrant behaviours that landed him in the insane ward of a hospital. He stands thus as the exact opposite of Ragin. The doctor, who considers it futile to pretend to cure, since it is

[13] *Ward No. 6.*

society that is ill, is answered by the patient, who himself blurs the boundary between health and illness, and between the world of free men and that of those locked away. Both bear witness to the perfect reversibility between inside and outside, between the hospital and the society it serves, the former being the simple reflection of the latter. This is why Ragin will suffer the same fate as his patient. He will be interned as a result of an initiative that suffices to prove his madness to his colleague and to society: one day he crossed under his own steam the boundary separating health from illness by taking the initiative to talk to this madman whom he ought simply to maintain in confinement and by discovering in him the only man in town capable of reasoning.

But the conversation with the madman not only ruins Ragin's reputation as a rational man. It also ruins his reason itself, his resignation to social fate and to the inevitable misfortunes of the times. In vain does Ragin preach to Gromov about the need to resign himself to an evil that has its roots in society and the times, and to seek refuge in the inner freedom of the wise man who understands the reason for things and scorns social contingencies. Gromov knows, as he does, that it is pure chance by which the one comes to occupy that place of the doctor and the other that of the madman. Only, unlike him, he does not find this 'chance' normal. And he rejects the easy philosophy that asks the victim of injustice to withdraw to the inner fortress of the wise man: 'We are kept here behind barred windows, battered, left to rot; but that is very good and reasonable, because there is no difference at all between this ward and a warm, snug study. A convenient philosophy. You can do nothing, and your conscience is clear, and you feel you are wise. . . . No, sir, it is not philosophy, it's not thinking, it's not breadth of vision, but laziness, fakirism, drowsy stupefaction.'[14]

We would gladly make the madman Gromov the spokesman for the writer and doctor Chekhov, who believed in science and rebelled against those who put up with servitude. But, once again, this writer does not work with the help of spokespeople; he works by constructing speech devices and conflicts between reasons that respond to each other from near and far and receive light and shade from their environment. The experience of the learned Doctor Ragin, which refutes from a

[14] Ibid.

distance the experience and progressionist faith of the scientist-engineer Ananyev, is refuted at its very place by the reason of the madman Gromov. But the turnstile of reasons does not stop there. The reasonable rationalism of the former and the paranoid over-rationalism of the latter are put on hold by the very form of the narrative, which precludes the victory of any speaker. *Ward No. 6* ends only with Ragin's death, which proves nothing for or against his philosophy. And *Lights* ends, without concluding the debate, with a confused vision of this construction site of progress at the centre of which presides a stupid dog: 'As I got on the horse, I looked at the student and at Ananyev for the last time, at the hysterical dog with the lustreless, tipsy-looking eyes, at the workmen flitting to and fro in the morning fog, at the embankment, at the little nag straining with its neck, and thought: There is no getting to the bottom of anything in this world.'[15]

This may be the conclusion the visitor draws, but it is not the end of the story. In truth, it does not end. Or rather, it ends with a beginning, like that of any day: 'The sun began to rise.'

[15] *Lights.*

**A New Dawn?**

Reasons can be turned around endlessly, the exemplary jousts for such turning Chekhov established in a few typical scenarios. There are the reasons that indignant people like Gromov pit against the satisfied, the resigned or the cynical. There are those that the sceptical student levels at the progressive Ananyev. But more often than not, the debate sets two kinds of progressives against one another. There are those – above all feminine – progressives whose concern is to improve the condition of the people through work, science and philanthropy. Such is the case of Lida, the heroine of *The House with the Mezzanine*, who sets about creating schools, libraries, dispensaries and pharmacies, and even teaches people at home. On the other hand, there are those who reject these material improvements because they only create additional needs and new forms of servitude. Instead of elementary schools and hospitals, they want people to be given the means to free themselves from work and devote themselves to the life of the mind. Lida's neighbour, a painter, also reasons this way against her. This is also, in *My Life*, Dr Blagovo's reasoning: educated people who want to share the life of the people would do better to develop their skills as scientists or artists to work for the spiritual progress of humanity and the great X that awaits it in the future. To which his interlocutor replies that among the things that 'progress', enslavement must also be counted.

Reasons get turned around endlessly, whereby reasons for progress get inverted into reasons for servitude. But only servile souls draw the conclusion that all is vanity and that all situations and actions are equal. The debate ends without a conclusion. Yet something remains, something that is fixed in the mind and able to serve as a compass: moments, sensations, lights, images. From a night of discussions, the anonymous visitor to the railway site drew the sole conclusion that the reason of the world could not be gotten to the bottom of. But his memory, for its part, has retained two impressions that are given to us together: the spectacle of light and the image of Kisochka. What is the connection between the two? This question is one that the reader shares with the student nihilist. The latter was unable to see how the seduction of even five hundred Kisochkas could prove anything about progress in history and the privileges of experience. And the reader him- or herself wondered how this banal story of a woman seduced and abandoned could gainsay the thesis of the nihilist student. The answer can now be given. Despite its apparent disproportion, the banal little story is well placed to respond to the thesis of the ultimate meaninglessness of life. But it does not respond simply by denouncing the story's moral outcome: the equivalence of good and evil that turns out well for the cynics. It does so by highlighting what lies at the heart of the whole affair: the use of time. What stands opposed to the great theses on the destiny of civilizations is the attention given to what it is that is happening in a given moment. The engineer sums up the whole affair in one sentence: 'What was for me an ordinary amatory episode was for her an absolute revolution in her life.'[16]

This is the young Ananyev's error, and the real reason why his banal story argues against the nihilist vision. His mistake is that he did not perceive, did not want to perceive, what was at stake for Kisochka – and for him too – in that moment. He adopted the ordinary morality of the male

[16] *Lights.*

seducer: there is only the shared amusement of a moment, and only the naivety or bad faith of a companion who has read too much literature and wants to see it as the entering into a new life. But behind the irony about women who transform some extramarital affair into a revolution of existence, there is something more radical: the refusal to believe in the very possibility of such revolutions. For the reasonable man, time can only ever contain the ordinary: there is the ordinariness of serious occupations and there is the ordinariness of pastimes, of which little amorous impromptus are a part. The power wielded by the seducer is thus nothing more than submission to the ever-similar time of serf consciousness. On this point, the nihilistic student is right against the teacher: the experience of age has absolutely no bearing here; it only ever reproduces the same submission to what is, the same agreed division between a time for serious things and a time for amusements. But, conversely, the naive Ananyev is right to fixate on this little story and on the decisive moment when he refused to see what was at stake in poor Kisochka's illusions: an unprecedented opening, the possibility of a breach in the ordinariness of time, of that new beginning of which all life is capable in an attempt to reach its truth.

For a moment is not only that which passes, the indifferent element of a duration that is always similar to itself. It can also be a pause, an opening, a glimmer of light that indicates the possibility of another life. 'Nothing passes away without leaving a trace', says the unhappy hero of *My Life*, 'every step we take, however small, has significance for our present and our future existence'.[17] It was this breakthrough from another time, this call of a life to come, that the young Ananyev could have seen in what was for him only the illusion of a naive lover. The 'absolute revolution in her life' that Kisochka sees belongs to those flashes of light that, in Chekhov's stories, pierce the time of servitude to point to the distant future of another life. The flashes arise in situations and among individuals greatly diverse in nature. Whether it is the constables in Dreams, who seem to forget their duties for a time to share with the tramp a vision of the great open spaces of Siberia. Or the nameless hero of *The Story of an Unknown Man* at the moment he gives up the domestic job he

[17] *My Life.*

had taken on to serve his revolutionary projects: 'I was ready to embrace and include in my short existence every possibility open to man. I wanted to speak, to read, and to hammer in some big factory, and to stand on watch, and to plough.'[18] Whether it was the alcohol-stupefied peasants of the village of Zhukovo (*The Muzhiks*) who found themselves shaken for a time by the procession of the icon of the Virgin Mary, source of life: 'All seemed suddenly to realize that there was not an empty void between earth and heaven, that the rich and the powerful had not taken possession of everything, that there was still a refuge from injury, from slavish bondage, from crushing, unendurable poverty, from the terrible vodka.'[19] Or the old believer Yakov Ivanitch on transhipment duty in Sahalin prison, where he is atoning for the murder of a brother he killed out of religious fanaticism: 'His eyes were dimmed with tears; but still he gazed into the distance where the pale lights of the steamer faintly gleamed, and his heart ached with yearning for home, and he longed to live, to go back home to tell them

[18] *The Story of an Unknown Man.*
[19] *The Muzhiks.*

there of his new faith and to save from ruin if only one man, and to live without suffering if only for one day.'[20] But it is undoubtedly the vision of *The Teacher of Literature*, Nikitin, that gives this call for another life its most complete formulation:

> He thought that, apart from the soft light of the ikon lamp, that beamed upon their quiet domestic happiness, that apart from this little world in which he and this cat lived so peacefully and happily, there was another world. . . . And he had a passionate, poignant longing to be in that other world, to work himself at some factory or big workshop, to address big audiences, to write, to publish, to raise a stir, to exhaust himself, to suffer. . . . He wanted something that would engross him till he forgot himself, ceased to care for the personal happiness which yielded him only sensations so monotonous.[21]

This other life is not about an upheaval of social positions; it's about breaking away from an existence that is always ready to take pleasure in its slavery. That's why the call is felt by

[20] *Murder.*
[21] *The Teacher of Literature.*

the rich merchant or the respectable professor as much as by the vodka-stupefied peasants. There is something that escapes the simple repetition of time: the individual life that each person is given only once. But there is also something that goes beyond individual happiness, whether it be that of strong alcohol, a high social position or a loving marriage. This intensification of life can be brief or long, it can consist of suffering or no longer suffering; it can be found by working with one's hands in a factory or by professing from the top of a university chair. It is not the satisfaction of a personal ambition, but the effort to escape the 'sensations so monotonous' of personal happiness, to escape the world that is satisfied with these happinesses alone.

It's called, in two words, the 'new life'. This expression resonated strongly in the Russia of the day, where it expressed the aspiration for a future in which servitude will truly have disappeared. *Novaya Jizn* was the title of the first organ of Russian social democracy, before becoming the watchword of the new revolutionary world and then the official slogan of Stalinism. In these two words are concentrated the more or less clear or confused visions of a world in which social justice will go hand in hand with individuals' ability to live a wider and more authentic life. And no revolutionary would disagree with the dream of the bride who, on the eve of her wedding, has fled a house where four servants sleep on the kitchen floor: 'if only that bright new life would come quickly, then one could face one's destiny boldly, cheerful and free in the awareness of one's right!'[22] But on the road to this future, the same revolutionaries would ask an insistent question, *the* question of the time: what is to be done (chto delat)? This is the title of Chernyshevsky's 1863 novel, which inspired a whole generation of revolutionaries and was wittingly taken up by Lenin in his famous 1902 pamphlet stigmatizing the two great vices of economism and spontaneism. It is also the question that Chekhov's characters never stop asking, or asking themselves. And, of course, the very modality of the question is different, not only because Chekhov is not a revolutionary and does not believe in revolution in Russia, but also because he is first and foremost a writer, a man who perceives the different meanings of a word and the different intonations of an

[22] *The Fiancée.*

expression. For Lenin, 'what is to be done?' was a univocal question that called for a choice to be made between contradictory answers. But for the writer Chekhov, who sees words incarnated in bodies, the contradiction is already at the heart of the question. 'What is to be done?' can mean two, exactly opposite things: by which means can the present order of things be changed? But also: what can be done about it? In other words: there is nothing to be done; nothing will change. This is the wisdom spouted by cynics like Orlov, the disillusioned 'liberal' in *The Story of an Unknown Man* who scoffs at his mistress's dreams of a new life and responds kindly to his accuser's diagnosis: 'Yes, my life is abnormal, spoilt, no good for anything, and I am prevented from starting a new life by cowardice – you're absolutely right there. But the fact that you take it to heart so, worry and fall into despair – that isn't reason, there you are completely wrong.'[23] But it is also the resigned wisdom of the doctor Ragin or his colleague, Astrov, who, in *Uncle Vanya*, mocks the 'new life' mentioned by his friend and justifies his mockery with a decisive statement: for a new life

[23] *The Story of an Unknown Man.*

to be conceivable, there would have to be more than two honest, intelligent men in the district. For science to change society, society would have to have already changed. And the same could be said of revolution.

This diagnosis leaves us with little to expect from the actions of the only revolutionary we encounter in Chekhov's short stories, the unnamed hero of *The Story of An Unknown Man*. He is, in fact, a very strange revolutionary, since we never see him take any actions or make any remarks of a revolutionary nature. No doubt there is a reason for this: his true identity, his commitment and his thoughts must remain unknown for the very success of his action. He has signed up as a servant in the service of the cynical Orlov, with a very specific intention: Orlov is the son of a famous statesman whose plans and intentions he hopes to learn about, probably in order to prepare an attack. Well, one day, alone at home, the statesman unexpectedly comes to visit his absent son. For the phony servant, it is the perfect opportunity to carry out his plan by eliminating his enemy and disappearing incognito. But he finds himself unable to seize the moment. The old man's sad face and the decorations on his chest inspire in him, in terms of hatred of the powerful, only conventional thoughts about the fragility of everything earthly. It is as if he has been seized by the nihilistic wisdom of the student Von Schtenberg, who renders all action derisory in the face of the death that awaits individuals and societies. But the way the story unfolds reveals that it is not philosophy that is staying his hand; it is simple adherence to the condition that he thought he had chosen as a means to an end. It's a strange idea to become a servant in order to fight against servitude. Chekhov's predecessors – Dostoyevsky, Leskov, Goncharov – had portrayed the revolutionaries they feared as fools or rogues. Chekhov, who has neither love nor hate for them, focuses on the very form of the revolutionary plot as conceived by the nihilist generation, and denounces its fundamental contradiction: the dissociation of means and ends. The relationship between the revolutionary end (the destruction of domination) and the means (the domestic service of a senior civil servant) is in fact a non-relationship. In the physical appearance of an old man visiting his son, the underground revolutionary is unable to recognize his intended target. And the energy he vainly seeks in order to act has been devoured by the months spent brushing his master's clothes, dressing him and taking letters to his mistress's house. Not only will he give up his plans, but he will be unable to answer the call from Zinaida, Orlov's neglected mistress. She had seen in her affair the beginning of a new life. When the underground revolutionary reveals himself and her lover's betrayal to her, she leaves with him, believing that he can guide her towards a new future. But when she asks him, 'What is to be done?' – the last question she asks him before she gives birth and commits suicide – the disillusioned revolutionary can only answer with a shrug of the shoulders. The only revolutionary Chekhov presents leaves the stage without having undertaken anything and returns the question 'what is to be done?' to its sceptical side: as his employer, the 'liberal' Orlov, used to say: '*well, what can be done?*'

This is where the 'naivety' of women in love prevails over the irony of liberals and the strategic calculations of revolutionaries. It rejects the separation of ends and means. The new life, the free and true life, cannot be the product of servitude and lies. To break the circle of servitude, the activities of today must already be implementing the principle of future life.

How can we grasp this anticipation of the future in the present? We can sense the need for it in the aspirations of women, but it is rather from another angle that one will, at that time, look for the answer. It can be found in a figure whose weighty and obscure activity seems to carry the positive force of a world to come: the worker. Being a worker, wielding a hammer, working in a big factory, no longer experiencing the long evenings of the idle – this is the dream that runs through the brain of the literature teacher and the underground revolutionary, just like that of the idle officers who frequent the salon of the *Three Sisters*: 'Man should work and toil by the sweat of his brow, whoever he is – that's the whole purpose and meaning of his life, his happiness and his joy',[24] says Irina, the youngest of the sisters. And her lover, Baron Tuzenbakh, goes even further. For him, work is not just an individual need; it is a new age in history: 'The time has come, something enormous is advancing

[24] 'Three Sisters', in *Five Plays*, trans. and introduced by Ronald Hingley (Oxford: Oxford University Press, 1977), p. 173.

toward us, and a formidable and beneficial storm is brewing; it is underway, very close, and soon it's going to sweep out of our society all the laziness, indifference, prejudices against work and morbid boredom. I'm going to work, and in twenty-five or thirty years' time, everyone will work. Everyone!'[25]

Tuzenbakh will be killed in a duel before leaving for his brickworks and marrying Irina. Hence, he won't have to experience the gap between work as the historical power of the world to come and work as an everyday occupation. It is this gap that is dramatized in *The Cherry Orchard* through the confrontation between Peter Trofimov, the revolutionary student, and Lopakhin, the son of a serf who has become a capitalist. In a beautiful tirade, Peter proclaims the necessity of work for the triumph of truth. Lopakhin reminds us that he gets up before five in the morning and works until the evening. He presents himself as the true worker, the one who creates the conditions for a better life, even in the modest form of summer houses. But Chekhov entrusts another character with the task of confronting *the* essential contra-

[25] 'Three Sisters', in *Five Plays*, p. 174.

diction here: how can one be both the worker of the present and the worker of the future? This character is Misail, the anti-hero hero of *My Life*. Under this title, we should obviously not expect a *Bildungsroman* that shows us how the son of a nobleman becomes determined to be a worker. None of Chekhov's stories begins with his hero's childhood. And none of his characters applies any theories. Theories are never more than comments from the outside on what they are experiencing. The 'life' that Misail tells us about begins abruptly in the middle. And this beginning is itself a scene of pure comedy: his dismissal from the ninth position he had been awarded, despite his proven incapacity, thanks to the fame of his father, the town architect. After a temporary job as a telegraph operator on a building site, Misail became a house painter. His story is often seen as a critical illustration of Tolstoy's call to share in the life of the people. Yet the way the story is told leaves little room for the character to be ideologically motivated. Misail becomes a labourer less out of philosophical conviction than through a combination of circumstances, primarily due to his inability to fit into the logic of the office jobs that would land him a career in the state nobility, where he has, however, never perceived anything but the monotony of mechanical and utterly useless work. In a sense, it was a simple matter of fact for him: excluded from the career of so-called intellectual jobs, he considered himself reduced to the ordinary condition and obligation of all those who earn their living by working with their hands.

But, for the defector that he is, this ordinary life soon appears to be the site of a twofold discrepancy. On the one hand, it is akin to simple daily necessity, which removes from work all value and even any particular meaning: 'I was living now among people to whom work was obligatory, inevitable, and who worked like cart-horses, often with no idea of the moral significance of labour, and, indeed, never using the word "labour" in conversation at all.'[26] But, on the other hand, the scandal caused by Misail's social decline made him, for members of his original class, especially if they had read Tolstoy, the apostle of a morality and of a religion of manual labour. His black hands and the smell of turpentine he carried with him made him a hero of the new life for the daughter of the same engineer

[26] *My Life*.

who had given up his job as a telegraph operator. She will make of him her husband, but she will also force him to improve his exemplariness, to become more like the man of the future that he embodies for her: 'Besides, you have often said yourself that everybody ought to earn his bread by the work of his own hands, yet you earn money and not bread. Why shouldn't you keep to the literal sense of your words? You ought to be earning bread, that is, you ought to be ploughing, sowing, reaping, threshing.'[27] Misail, who didn't like working the land, became a farmer to fulfil his wife's ideal and apply the instructions in her agronomic manuals. Farm life and relations with the peasants soon prove to be far removed from the idyll dreamt of by the engineer's daughter, and she ends up leaving Misail and returning to a worldly life embellished by artistic dreams. But before she leaves, she draws from their exemplary experience a lesson in dialectics that no Marxist would disavow:

> We have done a lot of work, a lot of thinking; we are the better for it – all honour and glory to us – we

[27] Ibid.

> have succeeded in self-improvement; but has our personal progress had any perceptible influence on the life around us? Has it brought any benefit to anyone whatever? No. Ignorance, physical uncleanliness, drunkenness, an appallingly high infant mortality, everything remains as it was, and no one is the better for your having ploughed and sown, and my having wasted money and read books. Obviously, we have been working only for ourselves and have conceived of wide-ranging thoughts only for ourselves.[28]

This is how the whirligig of reasons works: so as not to betray the new life, you have to be the man of the future right now. But by being the man of the future now, you are only ever working to perfect yourself. The dialectician will go out into the world, convinced, like the nihilistic student, that everything passes away; Misail will return to the condition of a simple worker, even if it means becoming a skilled and respected entrepreneur.

For the dialecticians of revolution, the moral of the story is easy to draw: you do not build the future by becoming a worker. You build the future by organizing the collective strength of the

[28] Ibid.

working class. The time of the apostles who went to the people to share in their condition is over. The role of defectors from the upper classes is now to organize the collective struggle to overthrow the capitalist system. The story of Misail's misadventures appeared in October 1896. Eighteen months later, the Russian Social Democratic Workers' Party was founded in Minsk.

**The Power of the Moment**

This is the conclusion of dialecticians. But this writer is not a dialectician. That means, first of all, that he does not draw conclusions. Misail's story proves nothing. And the story has no conclusion, at most an ending, which is itself homogeneous with the continuity of the story: it is a moment that follows others and does not say what will follow. This moment is that of a Sunday when the resting worker, with his niece in his arms, visits the cemetery where his sister, the child's mother, lies, and meets a friend of hers with whom he takes a few silent steps.

For Misail's story, at the moment it ought to have stated its moral, undergoes a bifurcation: it starts to bear less on him than on his sister, Cleopatra. Cleopatra had long been the embodiment of obedience to her father and to domestic order. One day, however, her friend Anna and her friend's brother, Dr Blagovo, took her on a picnic to the village where Misail worked, and she sensed in the cheerfulness of this part of the countryside the breath of another possible life. Little by little, her brother's example and the doctor's fine speeches about the greatness awaiting humanity in the distant future distracted her from her destiny as a housewife. When she becomes the doctor's mistress and becomes pregnant by this married, family man, she is rejected by the good society of her town and dies after giving birth to this fatherless child. Cleopatra thus seems the exemplary victim of the great theories about the new life. And yet she is the only entirely positive character in the story, the only one who acts according to her choice and shows no regret. She never ceases to declare herself perfectly happy with the irreversible break that has occurred in her life, and to bless the man who has dishonoured her in the eyes of the world and abandoned her to her fate.

The 'victim' Cleopatra is therefore, far more than her brother, the positive heroine of the new life, the one who 'looked her destiny straight in the eye'. And it is this exemplarity that gives meaning to the final episode of the story in which Misail meets Anna, the doctor's sister and Cleopatra's friend, at his grave. Anna does the complete opposite of Cleopatra. She has spent her life loving Misail from afar, without ever daring to declare her love or associate her life with that of a man ostracized from good society. Even today, she takes a few steps by his side, caresses the little girl with him, who for a moment can dream of being in the company of a father and mother, then leaves him at the entrance to the town. It is as if, beyond Misail, the end of the story is about two women: one who has dared to look her destiny in the face and one who has not. That's as far as the story goes. This is also what it means not to be dialectical: not to dissolve the opposition into a new figure that synthesizes and transcends it, to keep it alive in its place and time: that of the moment of choice, which is also the choice of one time against another: the openness carried by the moment against the continuous time of repetition. Cleopatra and her friend Anna embody this opposition between two ways of experiencing a quiet afternoon in the countryside: as a pleasant pastime or as the beginning of a revolution in existence, one that takes it from the 'rough draft' to the 'clean copy'.[29]

There is no dialectical overcoming. Everything happens at the beginning. And the beginning never ceases to replay itself. There is a choice, always the same: a threshold that you cross or do not cross to break the ordinariness of the pact of servitude. Here the view we must adopt is the exact opposite of the cynics'. They make fun of women who need to transform a love interlude into the beginning of a new life. The example of Cleopatra turns the argument on its head: what gives these women's loves their strength is that they go far beyond the attraction of a person and the pleasure they are capable of giving you. These loves are a war declared on a whole world of servitude, on a life forever busy with sugar supplies or salting cucumbers; they are a farewell to a world where, until death, 'one never stops lying, and tormenting one another, and one fears liberty and hates it as a deadly foe'.[30]

Hence the solid link that the writer forges between two things that seem to bear no propor-

[29] *Three Sisters.*
[30] Ibid.

tion to one another: the call for this new life, in which everyone is aware of their rights, and these little stories of avoided or unrecognized love, the versions of which he varies ad infinitum while building them around the same centre: the moment when it was – or would have been – possible to look one's destiny in the face.

This privileged moment can be a matter of pure chance. Such is the singular story of *The Kiss*. An officer, Captain Ryabovich, and his companions find themselves invited by the great landowner of the village in which they have made a stop. As he searches for his way through a darkened room in the castle, he is met by a woman who kisses him lovingly, mistaking him for a moment for the man she has been impatiently waiting for. Upon returning to the light of the living room, he was unable to identify the stranger and, when the regiment passed through the village again, he missed the opportunity to 'see again' the woman he had in fact never seen. On the banks of the little river that flows 'without knowing where or why', he will only be able to remember 'how fate in the person of an unknown woman had accidentally caressed him', and this memory is enough to make his life seem 'extraordinarily barren, wretched and drab'.[31]

But usually the encounter with fate, its acceptance or avoidance, are events that have the will – or lack of it – come into play. There is the accepted encounter, exemplified by the heroine of Chekhov's last story, *The Fiancée*. On the eve of her wedding, after visiting the flat that her stupid fiancé intends they use for their marital bliss, in which he has hung a painting by a fashionable painter of a naked woman next to a vase with a broken handle, she decides to flee as soon as possible. But, more often than not, the characters flee the moment at which they have to face up to their destiny. There are the cynics, like Ananyev and Orlov, who see their mistresses' dreams of a new life as a passing amusement. But above all there are those who are afraid, who shrink from an upheaval of their perceptible universe. Such is the case of the young statistician Ognyov in *Verochka*. He, too, is confronted with the call of a moment when, after several weeks' study, one August evening he decides to leave the home of the chairman of the Rural Commission. The air

[31] *The Kiss.*

is heavily scented with mignonette, tobacco and heliotrope. And the young man is savouring the results of his stay. He had enjoyed the welcome he had received from the host and had collected useful documents for the thesis he would be defending in Petersburg. There was just one minor mishap that disturbed his serenity. The daughter of the house, Verochka, offers to walk him back to the woods. As he is leaving, she confesses both her love for him and her desire to leave behind an aimless life spent among people with full bellies and to go to what she calls 'those great big damp houses of yours, where people are suffering and ground down by hard work and privation'.[32] For Ognyov, this attraction to the wretched is unserious sentimentality, and, as for this love, he searches in vain for the spark that could respond to it. It is not that Verochka is without charm. It is just that he has neither the experience of life's upheavals nor the desire to gain such experience. So, he leaves the young girl to her impossible dreams of escape, even if it means feeling as soon as he does that the chance of happiness he let slip away will never come again.

[32] *Verochka.*

But the most significant case is the one in which the missed encounter cannot be attributed to any individual calculation, to any fault on the part of a character, but to the sheer inability to prolong the power of the moment. Such is the story of another summer evening when the unnamed heroine of the story set off on horseback to fetch the mail from the station with a holiday friend, Pyotr Sergeyitch, a prosecutor by profession (*A Lady's Story*). The threat of a thunderstorm, the smell of nearby rain and of cut hay, the young man's jokes, the worrying yet exciting prospect of getting drenched, the dream of sheltering in a deserted castle and of being struck by lightning, make the two people share a hilarity that fills him with enough audacity to declare his love while she is enjoying looking into his shining eyes and listening to the words of love that mingle with the sound of the rain. But after this evening of madness, during which the young man has been so playful and life has appeared to the young girl to be 'rich, varied, full of charm', nothing has happened. Holidays are holidays, holiday friends are holiday friends, and the wall of social difference has come down between the young aristocrat and the examining magistrate, who is ill at ease in the salons. The young woman, who is no longer young, is left with the feeling that her life has been lost, without really knowing whether she is annoyed with herself for having maintained this wall of social distinction or whether she is annoyed with the overly shy lover for not having shattered it. But perhaps their common fault was simply their inability to interrupt the normal flow of time, to respond to the call of raindrops and the smell of cut hay on a summer's evening.

The faint-hearted, like the cynics, have despaired of the new life in advance. It is the fact that they do not despair that lends the otherwise unedifying couple in *The Lady with the Dog* their exemplarity. At first, Gurov behaves like a cynic, taking advantage of a holiday encounter that was supposed to end without complications when he returned to the city. Anna's initial attitude was that of a fainthearted person who is ashamed of her moment of weakness and still prefers her sad life as the docile wife of a servile dignitary to the adventure of an illegal love affair. Yet both of them eventually give in to the call of the sea breeze and the golden light of summer evenings. They are reduced to clandestine meetings in a hotel room when she comes to Moscow on the pretext of seeing her doctor. So, there is nothing very exalting in the story of this sad affair. But it takes on a completely different aspect if we compare it to another, more or less contemporary, story, the one told in the short story titled *About Love*.[33] This is the confession of the impossible love that the narrator, the landowner Alehin, has for the wife of a friend. He did not think it possible to tear her away from her tranquil family happiness and secure social life and involve her in the difficulties of his condition as a small farmer burdened with work and always uncertain of tomorrow. It is only when he bids her a final farewell that he confesses to a love that turns out to be mutual. Alehin is certainly more reasonable and moral than the lover of the lady with the little dog. And Chekhov is no campaigner for free love. He does not hesitate, however, to include the story of this respectful lover in a trilogy of lost lives, alongside the fate of *The Man in a Case* and the derisory 'success' of the little civil servant Nikolai, who has spent his life saving to buy for himself in his old age the run-down property, wedged between a brick factory and

[33] *About Love.*

a bone-burning factory, where he can play the barin and eat the gooseberries from his garden (*Gooseberries*).

In the light of this trilogy, published a year earlier, *The Lady with the Dog* takes on its full meaning. Unlike Alehin, the adulterous lovers have refused to give up on the promise of new life, even though they know – and above all feel – that it is not there. And this is why the end of the story acquires a significance that goes beyond the story of one particular couple, and even beyond the simple framework of a love story, to speak of the possibility of free life in general. 'And it seemed as though in a little while the solution would be found, and then a new and splendid life would begin; and it was clear to both of them that they had still a long, long way to go, and that the most complicated and difficult part of it was only just beginning.'[34]

'*And* it was clear to them . . .'. It is customary to translate this phrase as '*But* it was clear to them . . .'.[35] This departure from the letter of the text

[34] *The Lady with the Dog*.

[35] Translator's note: This is truer of the French translations of this sentence from Chekhov's *The Lady with the Dog*. But

is no doubt justified by the desire to make the narrative more logical by contrasting the hope of a solution with the awareness that it is still a long way off. Yet this logic is not Chekhov's, in whose work the conjunction prolongs far more often than it opposes. It is the same opening of time towards a distant freedom that allows hope to coexist with uncertainty. One must clearly sense that a lucid life remains far off. And it is precisely because it is distant that one must persist in pursuing the beginning. Because there are no fixed stages between the beginning and the end, and above all because the beginning is not at the origin – it is a rupture, a turning point in the course of existence, a pivot whose destiny is replayed at every moment.

## The Music of the Narrative

Thus, the moral code of the characters is defined. But what about that of the story itself? What

while the English translations generally follow Chekhov here, it would be easy to do so by overlooking the significance of the logic of the conjunction 'and' in his work. The merit of the modification introduced by 'but' in the French translations that Rancière alludes to here is to oblige a reflection on Chekhov's choice of 'and'.

is a story that is able to give full intensity to these stories of lost lives and these glimpses of other possible lives? Perhaps another story from Chekhov's later years offers the first elements of an answer. *Ionych* is yet another perfect example of a life lost. Newly settled as a zemstvo doctor in a distant province, Dr Dmitry Ionych Startsev is welcomed into the cultured family of the town, where the father organizes amateur theatricals, the mother writes novels and the daughter plays the piano. He immediately falls in love with the young and pretty musician. But she rejects him: she wants to escape this provincial backwater, study in Moscow, and pursue a career as an artist. Four years pass, during which Startsev builds a large practice and grows stout. Meanwhile, the young 'Kotik' (Kitten) returns home, thoroughly disillusioned about her artistic talents, and tries to win back the man she had idealized from afar as the dedicated 'doctor serving the people'. But a brief encounter suffices to convince him that 'it's a jolly good thing I didn't marry her'.[36] He will henceforth cease visiting the family altogether, continue growing wealthy

[36] *Ionych*.

without knowing why, and lead a life which he himself says is not a life.

*Ionych* thus presents another tale of a life lost but also, more subtly, a small lesson in literature. During Startsev's first evening in the Turkins' parlour, the lady of the house reads a novel that she herself has composed. This novel tells of the philanthropic deeds of a young and beautiful countess who builds the three pillars of progress in her villages – hospitals, schools and libraries – and who also defies convention by falling in love with a wandering painter. The narrator tells us that she 'read a story such as never happens in life, and yet it was quite pleasant and comforting to listen to it, and such calm, delightful thoughts passed through one's mind'.[37] The lady finishes her reading, a silence falls, and in that moment, the refrain of a folk song sung by a chorus in a public garden drifts in. Yet the narrator says: 'That song expressed everything that was absent from the novel and that happens in real life.'[38]

One could extend this small episode in ways that Chekhov refrains from introducing himself:

[37] Ibid.
[38] Ibid.

what is far from real life is not just the edifying tale of a philanthropic countess invented by an amateur writer; it might also include the work of a socialist writer like Chernyshevsky's *What Is to Be Done?*, which similarly blends romance and activism, portraying revolutionary action as spearheaded by a young woman who establishes a model cooperative of seamstresses. The authentic socialist novel, like the imaginary philanthropic one, features characters who claim to pave the way for progress by breaking the cycle of repetition and servitude. But what they fail to shatter is the *homogeneous time* that sustains such servitude. Among them, time remains an indifferent medium in which the wills of characters are executed, wills that are only the embodiments of ideas.

To this homogeneous time, illustrated by the novels of the cultured lady, Chekhov contrasts the time of the folk song: a melody both self-contained and open to all resonances, condensing into a few minutes 'everything that exists in life', and above all, everything that time itself is made of – sensations, emotions, boredom, waiting, nostalgia and dreams. In its refrains, where sorrow becomes joy, the folk romance is the form that unites the two dimensions and two affects of time: the straight line of succession and the lines of flight traced by momentary breaches, the nostalgia for a faraway freedom (*qui est loin*) and the call of freedom that is in the distance. The song sung by the chorus in *Ionych* is not unimportant. It is one of the most famous Russian love songs, *Luchinushka* ('Little Torch'). The *luchina* is the fragile candle made from a long wood shaving that once lit peasant isbas. The song gives voice to a young bride struggling to light the *luchina* to welcome her beloved, who himself keeps her waiting all night long.

The small *luchina* romance thus combines a lesson in life with a lesson in literature. To those who refuse both to despair of life and to resign themselves to its simulacrum, it teaches constancy in the expectation of what is to come, very late perhaps, at the end of a night that is likely to be long. The novelist certainly believes that a time will come when people will no longer want to live as they pretend to live today. But he also knows that no date can be set for that time. He says it and makes his characters say it: in a hundred years, in two hundred years perhaps, people will understand that we can no longer go on living like this. That is why it is worth trying right now to make them see what they do not want to see. One of Chekhov's characters, the indignant brother of the egotistical gooseberry man, recommends taking a heavy-handed approach: every self-satisfied person ought to have a 'man with a mallet' standing at their door, ready to deliver blows to remind them that the misfortune that befalls others may one day befall them too.[39] But Chekhov does not write literature with a hammer. And he even disliked using too stark a light for what he wanted to show. He, too, preferred to use the *luchina*, whose fragile flame was a kind of anticipatory response to the 'Lenin lamp' that, in the 1920s, would symbolize the light of progress brought by industry to peasant homes. The writer's *luchina* does not bring awareness to the ignorant; it merely reminds us that there was a promise, the promise of a clear life, a life in which we will know why we are living. It makes the tears of sadness and those of consolation tremble in the same vibration.

For the problem is not to make people understand the causes of unhappiness, but rather to

[39] *Gooseberries.*

make them feel sadness otherwise. This is one of the things understood by the nobleman who became a worker in *My Life*: 'The thoughts and doings of living creatures are not nearly so significant as their sufferings.'[40] The writer with the *luchina* does not claim to be changing the mindset of his readers to steer them towards the action that will generate a fairer society. He wants to change the modality of their sufferings (*chagrin*), and for that to serve justice in the present. 'We must above all be just, and all the rest will be added unto us', he wrote to his publisher on his return from the Sakhalin prison camp.[41] But the writer's justice is far removed from the violence of the man with the mallet. It is essentially a matter of precision, and therefore a matter of music. You have to find the right tone to make the suffering (*chagrin*) of one palpable to all, and the misfortune of all to each. The sledge-driver in *Misery* had been trying in vain to tell his customers, who were always in too much of a hurry,

[40] *My Life*.

[41] *Letters of Anton Chekhov*, Selected, Introduced and with a Commentary by Simon Karlinsky, trans. by Michael Henry Heim (London: Harper & Row, 1973), p. 174.

about the misfortune that had just befallen him with the death of his son, and he could only find his horse as a confidant. The writer, on the other hand, wants this misfortune to be accessible to the ears and sensibilities of any passer-by, such as the tramp in *Dreams* who, when he has time, sits down in a corner, picks up a little five-kopeck book and enjoys weeping to his heart's content.[42] To make the story of tears of sadness shed tears of joy, writing has to become music. One of the writer's most bitter short stories, *Enemies*, makes this point by taking us on a tour of the room where a couple mourn their child's death: 'In the general stupor, in the mother's attitude, in the indifference on the doctor's face there was something that attracted and touched the heart, that subtle, almost elusive beauty of human sorrow which men will not for a long time learn to understand and describe, and which it seems only music can convey.'[43] It is this gentle music that the noble maiden Ilovaisky feels one Christmas evening in the inn that provides temporary shelter for travellers trapped by a snowstorm (*On The Road*). There

[42] *Dreams.*
[43] *Enemies.*

she hears the exalted Liharev recount the succession of misadventures to which the scientific, religious, socialist and patriotic passions that have made up his life have led him, while one hears her young daughter, forced to follow her father's follies, moaning: 'All that she had heard was ringing in her ears, and human life presented itself to her as a beautiful poetic fairy-tale without an end. . . . This voice of human sorrow, in the midst of the howling of the storm, touched the girl's ear with such sweet human music that she could not bear the delight of it, and wept too.'[44]

Turning misfortune into song and tears of pain into tears of joy: for many despondent souls this is an unacceptable aestheticization of misfortune that prevents us from understanding the reasons for it and seeking remedies. But Chekhov sees things quite differently. The fundamental misfortune is servitude. And there is no reason for servitude other than servitude itself. It constantly reproduces, in the great and the small alike, the manners, affects and thoughts that perpetuate it in return. To break the circle, to form people capable of transforming the call of new life into

[44] *On the Road.*

reality, we must first change our ways of feeling. It is this revolution in affects that the writer applies himself to achieving. To do this, he has to tell and modulate otherwise the story of misfortune, blending its accents with those of the distant call. He has to create a melodic sequence that stands up to the hum of servitude and sinks deeper than it into the sensible experience of human beings. It is this hard-won battle that another story of night, tears and joy tells of, and which is also a story about the story: *The Student*. The hero of this very short story, the young Ivan, son of a poor deacon and a student at a religious academy, returns from hunting on the evening of a dark and icy Good Friday. He has the overwhelming feeling that it was the same cold wind that blew at the time of Ryurik or Ivan the Terrible and that still blows today on the same misery, the same ignorance and the same suffering. He realized that 'All these horrors had been, existed now and would continue to do so', and that 'the passing of another thousand years would bring no improvement'.[45] However, a chance meeting and a brief evocation will reverse the course of his

[45] *The Student*.

thoughts. On the way home, he passes by a bonfire where an old woman and her daughter are standing. As he talks to them, he tells the story of another chilly night and another fire, the one that the apostle Peter used to warm himself by, and by which he had denied Jesus three times before bursting into tears at the thought of his betrayal. The widow must have heard this story the day before, at the ceremony of the Twelve Gospels. And yet she bursts into tears as if the student's unassuming account, taking up the words of the Gospel of Saint Matthew, had spanned the centuries of Russian misery and servitude that weighed on her shoulders to re-establish the older, deeper bond that allows a simple country woman to share the feelings and weeping of an apostle who lived nearly two thousand years before her. This communion of sorrows (*douleurs*) produces a revolution in the student's mind that translates into overflowing joy: he feels that all the events of human history are linked together by the same chain: not the chain of servitude that always reproduces its own necessity, but the chain of a more essential bond of solidarity, of a sensitive cord that allows anyone to vibrate to the sound of sufferings and joys that are not his own. Anyone who touches one end of the cord today hears the resonance of the other, and feels part of a history that is completely different from that of shared servitude. This is what the student feels:

> And he reflected how truth and beauty, which had guided human life there in the garden and the High Priest's palace and had continued unbroken to the present, were the most important parts of human life, and of the whole of terrestrial life. A feeling of youthfulness, health, strength . . . and an inexpressibly sweet anticipation of happiness, of a mysterious unfamiliar happiness, gradually took possession of him. And life seemed entrancing, wonderful and endowed with supreme meaning.[46]

If we are to believe Ivan Bunin, this short story was Chekhov's favourite.[47] The reader may be surprised: the story is minimal – a young man returning home tells two women the episode of the Passion least likely to arouse fervour. And religious symbolism is not the writer's strong point, as the tyranny of a devout father forever distanced him from Christianity. There is, however,

[46] Ibid.
[47] Bunin, *About Chekhov*, p. 44.

a reason for his predilection for this modest story. To understand it, we need to look at another story about religion that echoes it and in which he displayed all his talents as an enchanter, *Easter Night*. In it, a monk who acts as a ferryman across the river exalts in recalling the marvellous Akathists that a poor vicar from the monastery had written 'for his own delight', using the most tender words and the most evocative metaphors, so that 'every little line be adorned in all ways, have flowers in it, and lightning, and wind, and sun, and all things of the visible world'.[48] These Easter nights do not speak to us of the mysteries of religion, but of the power of writing, the power that consoles by allowing tears to be exchanged for other tears, and that turns the modest and often decried act of consolation into the active power of a human tradition capable of overcoming the apathy of lives doomed to servitude.

## From the Song of the Steppe to the Song of the Bittern

But is it really the writer's vocation to console those who suffer? Even if Chekhov has no spokes-

[48] *Easter Night*.

man, it is hard not to attribute to him sometimes the feelings he lends to his characters. So it is with the disillusioned thoughts expressed by the otherwise unsympathetic character Trigorin in *The Seagull*:

> I love this lake here, the trees and the sky, I've a feeling for nature – it inspires me, gives me a violent urge to write. But then I'm more than a landscapist, I'm a citizen too. I love my country and its people. As a writer, I feel I must discuss ordinary people, their sufferings, their future – science, human rights, all that stuff. So I do discuss it, all in great haste, with everyone furiously hounding me in all directions, while I scurry around like a fox with the pack snapping at his heels . . . and I end up believing that all I can describe is the landscape.[49]

The landscapist is the enemy denounced by all those who care about improving the condition of the people. The young progressive landlady in *The House with the Mezzanine*, who wants to educate the poor, set up dispensaries to treat them and drive out the corrupt members of the zemstvo to do so, makes no secret of her hostility to the

[49] *The Seagull.*

artist, who, while being in love with her younger sister, paints landscapes instead of depicting the people's wretchedness. As for Chekhov, the doctor, he fought against epidemics, took part in the zemstvo and got involved in establishing schools. But Chekhov the writer was still accused of the cardinal sin of indifference to the misery and suffering of the people. He certainly did not shy away from describing this misery and suffering, but he failed to sound the call to fight them. And he establishes them within an overall picture, combining the effects of the rising or setting sun, fantastically shaped clouds, shimmers of light on the water, the crunch of leaves underfoot and birds singing in the reeds.

But perhaps the opposition between a taste for landscape and an interest in the suffering of the people is a little simplistic. Perhaps the passion for the former feeds another way of being interested in the latter. To understand this paradoxical relationship, we need to take a fairly long detour through Chekhov's first long novella, written at a time when, having published five-hundred short stories in five years, he was beginning to take his work as a writer seriously. This novella, which inaugurates a different approach to writing, is precisely a story about a landscape, *The Steppe*: a travelogue that is well framed between its point of departure – a small provincial town – and its point of arrival – another small town where the merchant Kuzmichov is going to sell his wool and take his nephew Yegorushka to school. Nothing of what ordinarily structures a fiction occurs in this story: there is no dramatic event, no change of direction, no unexpected turn of events. The story even sheds the merchant along the way, who, in search of his buyer, is only found again only at the end, once the transaction has been completed. It is as if the space of the journey cancels out the story of which it was supposed to be the stage. What remains is the pure straight line that leads the child to the place he has no desire to go, and makes a landscape pass before his eyes that waits for neither him nor anyone else and cares for no action. The narration insistently confers on this world at a standstill, through which the travellers pass, the flaw that critics attribute to the narrator: indifference. In the landscape through which the carriage passes, all the things, plants, animals and beings seen as it passes seem to share the same characteristic: we do not know why they are there, they do not know why themselves and they do not have the strength to want anything. The wings of a mill turn endlessly and never seem to want to leave the scene. A drover watches the horse-drawn carriage pass indifferently; a young peasant girl lying atop a cart blocking the road barely raises her head under insult; a grasshopper lets itself be caught, fed and released with equal indifference; a solitary poplar stands, God knows why, on a hill in the middle of the plain; rooks hover over the withered grass to stave off boredom; a dog that has rushed towards the carriage stops halfway, as if wearied by the prospect of barking; and a kite stops in mid-flight and seems to meditate on the tedium of existence before resuming its flight 'without anyone understanding why it is flying and to what end'.[50]

The story that marks a break in the short story writer's output is therefore a limit-story that seems to replace actions guided by the human will with the inertia of things and beings that are there without reason. But this apparent desertification is also the principle of a new song. While the adults take a siesta in the warm hour, the idle Yegorushka hears a woman's voice singing

[50] *The Steppe.*

a song that is like a barely audible lament that seems to come from all sides, as if it were the steppe itself singing and trying to convince of its innocence and desire to live the very sun that is scorching it. This melancholy tune seems to make the atmosphere even heavier and Yegorushka tries to flee from it, but it is then that he discovers the singer, as if dissociated from her song: a peasant woman in a short petticoat, perched legs as long as a heron's, shaking a sieve from which white dust lazily floats down. Indifference has become suffering, suffering has become song, the song is shared between the steppe and the peasant woman at work, transforming sadness into gentleness.

This gentleness reigns undivided in another motionless moment that is the counterpart of this one: at the hour when, with the evening mist preluding the nocturnal darkness, the day's sorrows are forgotten and 'all is forgiven'. At this moment 'a cheerful, youthful trilling that cannot be heard by day rises from the grass, as if it cannot see in the darkness how it has aged; chirring, whistling, scratching – those bass, tenor and treble voices of the steppe – everything blends in one unbroken din and against the background of these sounds it is pleasant to reminisce and to be sad'.[51] This evening concert is followed by a ballet of shadows where the dark shapes cut out by the moonlight take on a fantastic aspect and merge with all the figures forged by the legends of the steppe, wayfarers' stories and nurses' folk tales. Everything transpires as if the landscape itself were being told or sung in a narrative-world in which the very distinction between reality and fiction is obliterated.

The same indistinction that characterizes the forms of the landscape also characterizes the stories exchanged on the stage by the wagon drivers with whom Yegorushka continues his journey. The sight of a cross very close to the fire where the men warm themselves in the night is an opportunity to evoke the crime it commemorates: the murder of two icon merchants who, at the inn, had boasted a little too much about their gains and were murdered on this very spot by a gang of reapers. The story of this murder is an opportunity for one of the carters, old Panteley, to evoke a personal memory from long ago: one night in an inn where he was spending the night with a rich merchant, he discovered a gang of brigands in the

[51] Ibid.

cellar, sharpening their knives for the purpose of slitting this merchant's throat, and managed to thwart their plans. This began a chain of 'reminiscences' that would endlessly include inn nights, brigands with sharp knives and miraculous rescues. These tales of 'lived' events turn out to be fictions that Panteley repeats, without it being clear whether he has heard them from others or invented them himself, even if it means confusing them, over time, with his real-life adventures. These stories are like shadows distorted by the moon. Even if he confuses reality, stories he has heard and pure fiction, the story is authenticated by the very configuration of the place and time: 'The wayside cross, the dark bales, the wide expanse of steppe and the destinies of those gathered around the camp fire – all this was in itself so marvellous and terrifying that the fantastic and the imaginary grew pale and blended into real life.'[52]

In this way, *The Steppe* stages a certain utopia of the story: a story similar to the place that produces it, made unimpeachable by the very impossibility of distinguishing between reality

[52] Ibid.

and fiction. For it is the reality of the bare plain and the accidents strewn about it, the presence of bodies in space, the noises that envelop them, the lights of day and the shadows of night that is itself transformed into a melancholy song and a fantastic vision, capable of engendering other visions and other endless songs. The landscape tells its own story as the suffering of everything under the sun, but also as the redemption of that suffering, its transformation into a unanimous song in which we believe we perceive, conversely, 'the triumph of beauty, youth, the thriving of strength and the passionate lust for life'.[53] This triumph is only disturbed by the feeling that it has happened in vain, that it is unfolding its richness without anyone benefiting from it because no one has been able to prolong its song.

It would appear difficult to view Chekhov as the singer that the steppe was waiting for in vain. This long lyrical narrative, which marks a break in his conception of the writer's craft and heralded a sequel, has in fact remained a hapax in his oeuvre. Yet it is reasonable to think that this story, which has no posterity, plays a decisive

[53] Ibid.

role in the rest of his work. It is as if it put the storyteller at the right distance from his subject, as if it drew, once and for all, the line where the famous gap between the indifferent landscape and the suffering of the people is cancelled out. By becoming a song of pain and consolation, the 'indifferent' landscape provides the model for the right tone to modulate these 'sufferings', at an equal distance from picturesque curiosity and propagandist declamation. It is to set this tone that the journey through this multitude of tiny, sensible events, the reason for which we cannot see, serves. In the night of the steppe, when the bird called the 'sleeper' cries 'I'm sleeping, I'm sleeping, I'm sleeping' and the owl goes from guffawing to hysterical weeping, we wonder for whom they are crying and who hears them.[54] But Chekhov's readers will find the answer to this enigma thanks to another bird that the author makes sing, also without reason, ten years later, in the blackest of his short stories, the one that most mercilessly describes the 'sufferings of the people', not just those they endure but those they inflict on themselves.

[54] Ibid., p. 37.

*In the Ravine* is set in a sinister valley reeking of factory waste and a village world corrupted by the most sordid interests. The young and beautiful Lipa, the daughter of a poor day labourer, has been married off to the son of a rich merchant. But her husband, caught up in an affair about counterfeit money, is sentenced to prison, leaving Lipa and her young child defenceless against the jealousy of her sister-in-law, Akssinia. In her rage against the 'convict', Akssinia pours a basin of boiling water over the child, who dies that very evening. Lipa leaves the hospital overwhelmed, with the body of her son in her arms, and sits by a pond where a woman, accompanied by a child, is watering her horse. In the evening light, this little pond is transformed into a fairy-tale landscape that seems to have fled from *The Steppe*:

> The sun went to sleep, covering itself with purple and gold brocade, and long clouds, crimson and lilac, watched over its rest, stretching across the sky. Somewhere far away, God knows where, a bittern gave a mournful, muted cry, like a cow locked in a barn. The cry of this mysterious bird was heard every spring, but no one knew what it looked like or where it lived. Up by the hospital, in the bushes just by

the pond, beyond the village, and in the surrounding fields, nightingales were pouring out their song. The cuckoo kept reckoning someone's years and losing count and beginning again. In the pond frogs called angrily to one another, straining themselves to bursting and one could even make out the words: 'You're also no different! You're also no different!' (*I ty takova! I ty takova!*) What a noise there was! It seemed as though all these creatures were singing and shouting so that no one might sleep on that spring night, so that all, even the angry frogs, might appreciate and enjoy every minute: life is given only once![55]

One might readily deem inappropriate the narrator's way of forgetting Lipa and the dead child to indulge in painting a chromo-style landscape and joking about frogs calling to one another and the cuckoo muddling its count. But the narrator knows what he is doing. He knows what literature can do: speak to and for those to whom life is given only once; and first and foremost, take

[55] *In the Ravine*. Translator's note: Chekhov aptly exploits the sonorous properties of Russian here, as he does on many occasions: stressing the final vowel *a* in the phrase *I ty takova! I ty takova!* yields a sound akin to the Russian sound used to imitate the croak of a frog.

seriously this seemingly banal phrase. Everyone else speaks of life as if it never ends. Religion promises a happy future life to those who endure the sufferings of this one, and Lipa, who is pious, might well find solace in that. But the writer who created her does not settle for that on her behalf. Revolutionaries promise to change the life of the people, but the life they speak of is endless, and their suffering people neither die nor are born. Chekhov passionately wishes that those living in a hundred or two hundred years might lead a different life. But the only way he believes he can contribute to that future is by addressing those who live here and now, who live poorly but could already learn to live better, to cherish every minute of this time granted only once. 'Wait in the name of what? Wait, when you haven't the strength to live, and yet you must live and want to live!' demands the brother of the man with the gooseberries, revolting against the wisdom of the contented.[56] Chekhov shares this urgency but does not think, like him, that it must be hammered home with a mallet. He prefers another bass solo, the one he heard from the suffering

[56] *Gooseberries.*

steppe, which ceaselessly sings without reason of the absence of reason for its sorrow, transforming it into confidence and joy. 'I'm sleeping, I'm sleeping! I'm sleeping!' sings the drowsy bird in *The Steppe*, accompanying the owl who shifts from laughter to tears and tears to laughter. In this muffled music, the steppe expressed a 'passionate lust for life',[57] a will without reason, like Schopenhauer's, but not painful and brutal as in his case: melancholy, no doubt, but with an irony-infused, cheerful melancholy. This blend of tones is certainly difficult to hear. And we know Chekhov never managed to convince actors and critics that the plays they saw as sombre tragedies were light comedies. Yet we can glimpse what he meant when he lets us hear, around the grieving Lipa, the cuckoo muddling in its counting, the frogs trumpeting their 'And you're no different!', and above all the bittern, that bull-voiced bird whose song shares the same qualities as the melancholy solo of the peasant woman that epitomizes the steppe's song: like hers, it comes from everywhere and nowhere. And this, too, is how literature can act today and now.

[57] *The Steppe*.

This harsh yet consoling song of the invisible bird, this song from everywhere and nowhere, addressing no one and everyone, offers an image of literary 'indifference' slightly richer, slightly more unsettling too, than the clichés of the artist's ivory tower and the aesthete's distinction. This writer is not the master thinker dispensing precepts to the builders of the future. Nor is he the solitary soul carving into marble for eternity. He is one who, with his now-anonymous song, accompanies a present life that must care, at every moment, to make itself more beautiful.

**The Soldier's Eyes**

What stories should we tell readers who are far from freedom but must keep their eyes open to its presence in the distance? And how should we tell them? Chekhov rarely gives lessons in poetics. But his characters occasionally do so for him in passing, while speaking of other things. And a double lesson in poetics is offered by the characters in an unassuming short story titled *Home*. A widowed father learns from the governess that she caught his seven-year-old son smoking. The father is a prosecutor by trade but also a progressive man who prefers persuasion over violence with a child still grieving his mother's death. He thus deploys, by turns, rational arguments to show the boy his wrongdoing and moral precepts to provoke shame. Little Seryozha listens to the reasons and reprimands without seeming particularly concerned. He does, however, remind his moralizing father of his own duty: to tell him a story, as he does every evening. The father has exhausted his stock of tales and is not adept at inventing plots. So, he improvises as he goes. His story unfolds through haphazardly strung-together scenes. It tells of a king from a legendary country who lives in a glass palace surrounded by a wondrous garden: tulips, roses and lilies of the valley bloom there; oranges, bergamots and cherries ripen; multicoloured birds sing and glass bells hanging from the trees chime delicately in the wind. But an unforeseen shadow threatens this paradise. The kind crown prince has only one flaw: he smokes. This leads him to contract tuberculosis and die at twenty. The old king is left defenceless against his enemies, who kill him and destroy his palace. The once-magical garden is left barren, with no cherries, birds or bells. The child is moved by this beautiful, sad tale and vows never to smoke again.

The moral of the story seems simple – even too simple: lecturing those who act wrongly is pointless. Better to tell them stories that speak of themselves under other names and let them draw their own lessons. Isn't this what the writer himself does to urge the people of his time to change their lives? But the matter is more complex. For it is not about sugarcoating a lesson that would otherwise be too bitter. The father, moreover, harbours no illusions: the child succumbed solely to the story's charm, to the desire to preserve the imaginary garden. Nor is it merely about using one emotion – the pleasure of fiction – to evoke another: shame towards one's own life, presented in the guise of a fable. It is about awakening a new way of feeling through the fusion of contradictory affects, or rather, through the invention of an affect poised on the boundary between opposites.

This, in a sense, is an age-old question, as old as the claim that depicting human vice or misfortune can instil virtue. Rousseau's dilemma is familiar: how can one inspire the horror of vice while making its representation pleasurable? One possible answer is to curtail the pleasure, to portray the vice of a society or social milieu so dark that it becomes unbearable to the reader or spectator. This is the approach of one of nineteenth-century Russia's leading writers, Mikhail Saltykov-Shchedrin. His bleak depictions of the Russian nobility are hard to endure. The disgust provoked by 'Little Judas', the sordid antihero of *The Golovliov Gentlemen*, is inescapable. One might think such revulsion could fuel hatred of the existing order and a desire to upend it entirely. Hence Saltykov-Shchedrin was honoured as a great forebear in Soviet Russia. But Chekhov does not believe in such consequences. He does not believe society can be radically changed through disgust at one's own life. Disgust remains a servile passion, breeding resentment more often than revolt. It is not resentful men who change life. It is those who have begun to feel, in a more just and harmonious tone, the failings of their own existence. The story that shames the men of this age must resemble the bittern's raucous yet consoling song: it must make them see, hear and feel their misery in a happier way, by making them cry twice – once for the shame they feel, and once for the consolation offered.

The question is how to do it. And here, too, the unassuming little story gives us some pointers.

If the father succeeds in convincing the child, it is without having wanted to, at the moment when he stopped wanting to, when he simply tried to please him with a nice story. But he also proceeded in a particular way: with improvised tableaux that follow one another haphazardly. This is certainly not exactly Chekhov's method. The episodes in his stories are not added onto one another according to the inspiration of the moment. But they do have one thing in common with the prosecutor Bykovsky's stories to his son: they are made up of tableaux that follow one another without anything necessarily linking them to the preceding and following ones.

Take, for example, the short story *Fear*. The narrator is visiting a couple of friends who often welcome him in the countryside. On Sunday mornings, he goes to the village with the owner of the house to buy zakuskis, meets a former servant of his, a good-for-nothing nicknamed 'Forty Martyrs', who clings to them and, while waiting for the carriage to take them back to the estate, listens to the confidences of his friend: he lives in fear because he has the feeling that he does not understand what is happening to him, day after day. In particular, he does not understand how he can live with a woman who once told him, to put an end to his advances: I don't love you, but I'll be a faithful wife. After a joyful dinner, the husband, who has to leave early the next morning, rushes off to bed. The narrator is left alone with the mistress of the house, who asks him not to force himself to keep her company. As he strolls through the garden, he hears Forty Martyrs moaning about his lost life. He decides not to waste the evening and passionately embraces his friend's wife. In the room he takes her to, she confesses her love for him and her desire to leave with him. As she leaves the room in the early hours of the morning, she comes across her husband looking for a forgotten hat. Her husband's only reaction is to declare once again that he does not understand what is happening to him. But now it is the narrator's turn to wonder why things have happened the way they have, what the hat is all about and who this story serves, before finally walking out of a house where the couple will continue their life together.

A series of microscopic events culminates in what could be a life-changing event for all the characters, but ultimately has no consequences for any of them. They are all 'tableaux', little episodes that do not form any necessary causal chain. Many of Chekhov's short stories present this structure: a continuum of time, made up of mornings, afternoons and evenings, where something happens that had no particular reason to happen, or, conversely, something could happen and doesn't. The good father improvised as he went along. But in Chekhov's short stories, life itself seems to be made up of successive improvisations. Reversals of fortune are as rare in Chekhov's work as ineluctable chains of cause and effect. His characters are not engaged in those great enterprises that expose them to reversals of fortune. They ordinarily live their lives on the edge of something and nothing, with two typical scenarios: something could happen but does not; something does happen but remains homogeneous to the ordinary course of things to no good purpose. These alternative scenarios are illustrated in two stories that are more or less contemporary: *With Friends* and *At Home*. In the first story, the lawyer Podgorin is invited over by friends whose scenario is reminiscent of *The Cherry Orchard*: their financial situation is catastrophic, their house is about to be sold and, to avoid this happening, they would like for him to marry the youngest member of the family. An exemplary scene shows Podgorin meditating in the night on a terrace at the foot of which the pretty Nadezhda, who earlier was twirling in his arms and who now prowls dreamily in the night, passes by. He could very well give her a sign of life, but he remains silent and the young woman, who had thought she heard a noise, leaves, convinced that no one is about, after which Podgorin hurries back to pack his bags. *At Home* presents us with the opposite situation. Back in the deep country after the death of her father, young Vera is horrified to find a province and a family where the habit of beating servants is still alive in people's minds. Her miserly aunt is determined to marry her off to the local rich man, the doctor and industrialist Neshtchapov. She has no attraction for him, but marries him in the end because, all things considered, she has no reason not to.

The one flees and the other remains. But each of them has renounced the possibility of a different life. This possibility sometimes plays out in a single moment. This is the case for Podgorin as it is for the hero of *Fear* or for the young statistician Ognev in *Vera.* The same story can play out over a few days that summarize an entire life, as in *Vladimir the Great* and *Vladimir the Small*, where the heroine Sophie initially expresses her turbulent joy as a young woman in love with the handsome older man she has just married – Vladimir the Great – before giving herself the next morning to her long-time love – Vladimir the Small – who will abandon her after a week, after which life will return to its usual course, and the two Vladimirs will continue their games of billiards and cards. The tale of almost nothing can also stretch over several months. This is what happens in *A Boring Story*, where the days in the life of the old professor follow and resemble each other, days divided between family routine, which is organized by a mediocre wife and daughter, and evening jaunts at his goddaughter's, a failed actress in the manner of *The Seagull*, to whom he is bound by a love that cannot be expressed, until that definitive farewell where the professor, awaiting death in a hotel room, hopes the young woman will look back as she leaves without turning around.

There are indeed, here and there, a few murderous outbursts, such as the basin of boiling water poured onto Lipa's child by a jealous woman, the bottle and the iron with which the old believer

Jacob's wife strikes her cousin Matvei on the head, or the arsenic that Mashenka in *Peasant Wives* administers to her husband, who made the unfortunate decision to return from service while she was living a good life with a lover more to her liking. There is also the absurd gunshot by which the young Volodia, in the eponymous short story, brings an end to his own days because the young woman he had the audacity to take in his arms gently mocked his fledgling career as a seducer. But these episodes of violence remain exceptions, even if Machenka's audacity inspires dreams in the two unhappily married young women who hear the story recounted by a passing traveller. The traveller will leave with his story, and life will go on as before for the woman whose husband cheats on her and for the one who cheats on hers.

There is a reason why such violent actions are rare in Chekhov's novellas. It is that episodes of major violence make use of strong causalities and calls for great explanations: for some, it is the miserable situation of the oppressed and ignorant people, the pressure of the social environment or the iniquitous condition imposed on women; for others, it is the neglect of religion, the criminal ideas introduced by subversive thinkers or the neuroses of a disordered society. Chekhov would have none of it. There are no causal links of a social, psychological or ideological nature that explain and justify the characters' behaviour. Once again, servitude is the sole cause of itself, and the individuals are solely responsible for a miserable life that they could make better. At each moment, it is up to them to choose between two formulas, which are two ways of dealing with time: *everything passes by or, on the contrary, nothing passes by, everything leaves behind its trace*. One follows the normal course of things or responds to the singularity of the moment when the call of another life is heard. This ethical commitment is reflected in the form of the story, made up of separate moments that follow one another without necessity, and which might just as easily be wholly different. Situations simply follow one another, rather than being explained by one another and disappearing into their causes. Instead of a cause-and-effect relationship, there is a succession of moments when something happens or else nothing does. Characters can choose to take the plunge, like Nadia, the heroine of *The Fiancée*, who leaves the family home. But what happens to her then is beyond the point where the story ends. Chekhov certainly sympathizes with the young woman, but his task is not to invent her future. It is to draw the line from which she herself chooses to undertake a deviation and to accompany it to the narrow edge along which the characters walk between something and nothing. This is why, in his work, the story is most often a simple possibility of a story – 'the introduction to a story', as the unhappy lover of the whimsical Ariadne puts it.[58] But it is by persisting on this edge that he intends to bear witness to a society and an era, in other words first and foremost to a way of living – or not living.

The claim appears disproportionate. But disproportion is itself the principle of a poetics. To understand this, we need to complete the 'poetics lesson' offered by *At Home*, but we also need to change teachers: it is now little Sérioja who must teach us. This child, who loves to draw, has attracted some apparently well-founded criticism from his father: he is neglecting proportions and has drawn a soldier who is taller than the house he is standing next to. But the child is undaunted and gives an unanswerable response

[58] *Ariadne.*

to the objection: if he had drawn the soldier to scale, we would not be able to see his eyes.

The priority is to see the soldier's eyes. And to do that, you have to accept the disproportion. Young Sérioja is apparently adopting an impressionist aesthetic. The narrator tells us that he reproduces not only the objects but also his sensations in pencil, and that he has his own ideas about the colours of the letters: he draws l's in yellow, m's in red and a's in black. Chekhov was not concerned with giving colours to letters, nor with the synaesthesia that would preoccupy artists of the Symbolist age. But he, too, thought that the important thing was to paint people's eyes, and that to do so one could neglect the proportions of well-stitched stories. To his brother, who was also trying his hand at composing stories, he always gave the same lesson: you can dispense with the *plot*, what counts is the *subject*.[59] For him, the subject is the little scene borrowed from everyday life, the little moment,

[59] Letter to A. P. Chekhov of 11 April 1889, in *A. Chekhov, Vivre de mes rêves. Lettres d'une vie*, trans. from Russian to French, Nadine Dubourvieux (Paris: Robert Lafond, 2015), p. 318. Translator's note: The quote has been translated into English from the French text.

a distillation of ordinary time, where we can see individuals who themselves are watching what is happening and feel the breath of servitude or the call of another life passing by. And it is the perception they have of their lives, their sensations, that he paints at any given moment. This is what gives his descriptions their special character: they give us little information about the domestic setting and furnishings among which his characters live. Instead, they wrap their sensations in the thickness of an atmosphere, the light of a sunrise or sunset, the play of clouds in the sky, the distant songs or the sound of bells at a particular time of day or night. And it is in this way that these small scenes show themselves capable of condensing a global reality with which they seem out of all proportion: that of a society, a time, a way of life.

One painting after another, one tonality after another. As is often the case with Chekhov, music offers a significant analogy. One of Chekhov's most inspired short stories, *The Reed-Pipe*, describes a meeting on a heavy, rainy day between the bailiff of an estate and an old shepherd. In it, the shepherd makes a long plea against the destruction of nature by man, a plea echoed by Doctor Astrov in *Uncle Vanya.* He is also a musician in his own way, playing a country pipe that he has made himself. But his music is very particular: 'They were using only five or six notes, drawing them out lazily and making no effort to combine them into a motif . . . The highest, shrillest notes, which trembled and then broke abruptly into sobs, as though the pipe were sick and frightened; whilst the lowest conjured the mist, the distressed trees and the grey sky.'[60] The bailiff, on hearing them, felt 'full of bitterness, a terrible sorrow at the thought of the disorder in nature'.[61]

The writer/landscapist no doubt shares this sadness. But he is even sadder about the disorder that exists in the way the humans around him live – or forget to live – the life they were only given once. The erratic thoughts and behaviour of his characters can resemble these long, drawn-out notes. But he is concerned, on his own account, to assemble them into a song. He is concerned to unite the accents of sadness with the melodic line of consolation. It is the same line that mingles

[60] *The Reed-Pipe.*
[61] Ibid.

with the accents of renunciation and resignation and introduces the promise of a possible happiness. The two typical scenarios of the one who flees and the one who resigns provide two versions with lighter or darker but equally soothing tones. Podgorin's silence towards the woman who is waiting for him in the night, promising him a happiness that is just around the corner but which he puts off, lets us hear, even in the mode of renunciation, the music of another, more distant but higher happiness:

> And now, as he sat there in that tower, he would have preferred a good fireworks display, or some moonlight procession, or to hear Barbara reciting Nekrasov's *The Railway* again, or that another woman was standing there on the bank where Nadejda was now standing; this other woman would have told him something absolutely fascinating and new that had nothing to do with love or happiness. And if she did happen to speak of love, this would have been a summons to those new, lofty, sensible forms of life, forms on whose threshold we are perhaps already living and which we sometimes seem to approach.[62]

[62] *With Friends.*

Vera's resignation to the greyness of a godforsaken hole and a loveless marriage is not accompanied by any promise of an as yet unknown happiness. But the story lulls her no less with the song of the steppe: 'Beautiful nature, dreams, music, told one story, but reality another. Evidently happiness and truth existed somewhere outside real life . . . One must give up one's own life and merge oneself into this luxuriant steppe, boundless and indifferent as eternity, with its flowers, its ancient burrows, and its distances, and then all will be well.'[63]

All will be well: we need to hear both the bitter irony of a sentence to be translated into its opposite and the sweetness of the music that accompanies it. The same suspension points echo Vera's burial in the indifferent steppe and the new forms of life that can be sensed in Podgorin's silence. In the very story of lives lost, the song maintains the promise that the characters have renounced.

[63] *At Home.*

## Without Beginning or End

The narrative bears witness to its own time and opens onto the possibility of another time, on two conditions that at first glance seem incompatible: the first is that it refuses to be explained by that time, that its own temporality has no outside; the second is that it refuses to close in on itself. Its unity is that of a fragile melodic line running through the discontinuity of episodes that no necessity links to one another. But it must also come from nowhere and fade away without coming to an end. It is this paradoxical requirement that is summed up in the quip of Chekhov's reported by Ivan Bunin: 'In my opinion, after one finishes a story, he should cross out the beginning and the end. It is here that we writers lie most of all'.[64]

Not lying is the absolute condition for writing to retain the measure of distant freedom. But in literature, lying is not about the veracity of the events recounted. It is about the modalities of their linkage. It is about the mode of temporality that ensures it. The great lie about time is the one that identifies it with necessity. And this lie

[64] Bunin, *About Chekhov*, p. 12.

happens to be perpetrated especially on beginnings and endings. The beginning is deceptive when it is identified with the starting point of a causal chain that explains the action and justifies the characters by putting social or psychological determinisms into effect. The ending is misleading when it implies that the action has come to an end and that nothing else could come of its unfolding. A writer committed to truth takes the action and the characters along for the ride and leaves them there. He paints things 'as they are', in other words, via the middle, without grafting onto them a beginning whose consequence they would be or an end to which they would necessarily lead. Chekhov's narrative never begins by telling us about the characters' previous lives or describing the milieu in which they live. More often than not, the naming of a time and place is enough to set the narrative in motion. 'It was already ten o'clock in the evening. A full moon was shining over the Shumin's garden, the service . . . had just finished.'[65] This is how *The Fiancée* begins. 'It was dark, but already lights had begun to gleam here and there in the houses . . . Laptev

[65] *The Fiancée.*

was sitting on a bench waiting for the end of the evening service.'[66] This is how *Three Years* begins. And *The Student* reduces the introduction to a minimum: 'At first, the weather was fine and calm.'[67] After a start like that, anything can happen.

But it is not enough for the starting point to be indifferent. It must also reject any previous history for which it is the point of arrival. Significantly, this requirement is most strongly imposed where the character best seems to embody a figure characteristic of the period. This is particularly true of *My Life*, the story of the fired son of a nobleman who becomes a factory worker. Contrary to what the title would lead us to expect, and to what we have become accustomed in the life stories that Chekhov's century was full of, Misail's 'life' does not begin at birth and tells us nothing about his childhood, the loss of his mother, his illusions or his sadness. It begins at a precise point in time with a comedic dialogue. To a superintendent who tells him that, without the regard for his worthy father, he would have sent him flying

[66] *Three Years.*
[67] *The Student.*

long ago, Misail simply replies: 'You flatter me too much, your Excellency, in assuming that I am capable of flying.'[68] It is with this joke alone that 'his' life begins, the life that the story will now unfold. Even more significant is the beginning of the story of the revolutionary without a revolution in *The Story of an Unknown Man*, which dispenses with any explanation of the situation in which we meet him: 'For reasons which it is not now the time to discuss in detail, it was necessary for me to become manservant to a certain official in St. Petersburg by the name of Orlov.'[69] But it is not only the reasons why he entered Orlov's service that remain unexplained. Far more radical are the reasons that made him a revolutionary and the actions he took as a result. He tells us in passing that Zinaida, Orlov's neglected mistress, rubbed her hands together at the story of his 'amazing adventures', but he does not say a single word about these adventures themselves.[70] The 'life' of the man with no name began with the first line of his story and will end with the last.

68 *My Life*.
69 *The Story of an Unknown Man*.
70 Ibid.

But the problem of the ending that is not an ending is far more difficult than that of the beginning. Of course, Chekhov's concern about how to end something that has no end is not unique to him. It marks an era that has abandoned the great novels of the conquering will, in search of social positions or unattainable women, in favour of the multiplicity of sensible events of which every life is woven. For all those who, like Flaubert, no longer believe in the great chains of cause and effect, it is foolish to want to draw conclusions. The fact remains that they have to put an end to what could go on indefinitely. There is the solution of the Conrad-style *coup de force*, in which an adventurer in *Lord Jim* or a noble father in *Nostromo* is commissioned to eliminate a hero who would otherwise continue wandering indefinitely. There is Flaubert's solution: the end, as silly as life itself, which confirms the futility of great dreams: the Turkish brothel, whose failed visit is the best time Frédéric and Deslauriers ever had; Bouvard and Pécuchet's return to copying; Homais' being awarded a cross at the end of *Madame Bovary*. Chekhov sometimes imitates Flaubert, for example in *A Woman's Kingdom*, where the heroine, after recalling the blessed time when she did not own a factory, contemplated various philanthropic actions, dreamt of marrying one of her workers and carry through, despite everything, the social niceties of the annual party, laughs and cries with her maid, who has had an unhappy love affair, at the futility of all their dreams of change: 'We are fools! Oh, what fools we are!'[71]

Chekhov even sometimes simply dismisses the 'end of the story', as in *Ariadne*, where the narrator tells us that he does not know how the sad story of the young woman's bruised lover ended. But while he shares Flaubert's or Conrad's conception of literary truth, Chekhov does not share the nihilistic vision they associate with it. If there is no end, it is not that everything passes and nothing has meaning; it is that freedom is always far away (*loin*) and always in the distance (*au loin*), and we must respect the distance that simultaneously separates us from it and summons us to it. He therefore opposes the stupid ending to the divided or suspended ending.

The former is exemplified by the end of *The Duel*. This long story centres on the hostility

[71] *A Woman's Kingdom.*

between two characters. The first is Laevsky, a lazy civil servant who has washed up in this port, on the run with a woman that he has snatched from her husband but now wishes to get rid of. Opposing this idler who plays the children of the century in the manner of Onegin, is the man of progress Von Koren, the learned zoologist who is here for his research, but is also a fanatical Darwinian who thinks that society should eliminate parasites like Laevsky. After the abortive duel in which he misses the chance to do so, the story will bifurcate. Laevsky makes amends, works to pay off his debts and marries his now widowed partner. Von Koren repents his intransigence. 'Nobody knows the real truth', he tells Laevsky before leaving him and setting sail.[72] This could be the last word, and Laevsky takes it as such. But as he looks at Von Koren's dinghy struggling to reach the ship in heavy seas, he sees in it a metaphor for humanity's march towards truth, which he sums up in a phrase that Lenin would take up with a twist some years later: 'Two steps forward, one step back.' 'And who knows?' he concludes, 'Perhaps they will reach the real

[72] *The Duel.*

truth at last.'[73] It is a second last word. But this metaphor of the future perceived in the dinghy's progress is immediately contradicted by the remark of one of the spectators, who prosaically observes: 'There's no sight or sound of them.' This would be a third last word. But it is not the end yet, because the story will end with the curtain falling, entrusted to an indifferent nature: 'It began to spot with rain.'[74]

The suspended ending is expressed more subtly, in a more condensed way, in the contradiction that a descriptive notation often brings to the logical conclusion of the story. The best example of this is the end of *The Story of an Unknown Man*: the hero – or anti-hero – of the story sets out to return to her natural father, the civil servant Orlov, the little girl in his care after the mother's suicide abroad. He loves the child, but he can't keep her because he's in the final stages of tuberculosis and has to ensure the little girl's future. Orlov has nothing to do with the child. Fortunately, he has an influential friend, the lawyer Pekarsky. Pekarsky is incapable of under-

[73] Ibid.
[74] Ibid.

standing anything to do with feelings. But he is capable of opening all the doors and solving all the problems of those who come to him. Orlov entrusts him with the task of finding a solution, and he soon writes to the hero that everything has been arranged: Pekarsky has found an institution that can take care of the child.

The story is thus closed, except for one last sentence that reopens it completely: 'I read this letter, and Sonya was sitting on the table and gazed at me attentively without blinking, as though she knew that her fate was being decided.'[75] Clearly, the child's gaze will do nothing to change her fate, since the hero is obliged to part with her. And nonetheless this gaze is enough to render the ending undecided. It contradicts the world of petty arrangements and gross cowardice in which the 'liberal' Orlov and his friend the resourceful Pekarsky are masters; it shines the light of another future in the one reserved for the little girl. The hero has finished his task; the child has been placed. But her gaze is not, and it will have the last word: a last word that says that nothing is finished, that freedom remains far off and in the distance.

[75] *The Story of an Unknown Man.*

This suspended ending takes on its full meaning by concluding – without concluding it – the story that pitted a cynical liberal against a bankrupt revolutionary. Confronting both progressives who claim to chart the paths of the future and nihilists who declare the futility of any future beyond a return to the dust of individuals and civilizations, Chekhov's writing obstinately traces an undecided opening of time. The free country remains distant, and the distance separating us from it can no more be measured than the road leading there. Yet this distance is also what binds us to it: what the characters in fiction dream of, what many abandon but others strive to cross in diverse ways, often with opposing outcomes. The writer neither shares nor condemns their endeavours or illusions. What specifically falls to him is to give this freedom the time of its immeasurable measure: this time moved through the relentless machinery of repetition, yet which, from pause to pause and from breach to breach, is torn and split into a time of anticipated freedom – a freedom that refuses the ending, the full stop, remaining a possibility in suspense. We may call this a politics of literature.